PHILO'S JEWISH IDENTITY

Program in Judaic Studies
Brown University
BROWN JUDAIC STUDIES
Edited by
Jacob Neusner,
Wendell S. Dietrich, Ernest S. Frerichs, William Scott Green,
Calvin Goldscheider, David Hirsch, Alan Zuckerman

Project Editors (Project)

David Blumenthal, Emory University (Approaches to Medieval Judaism)
William Brinner (Approaches to Judaism and Islam)
Ernest S. Frerichs, Brown University (Dissertations and Monographs)
Lenn Evan Goodman, University of Hawaii (Studies in Medieval Judaism)
William Scott Green, University of Rochester (Approaches to Ancient Judaism)
Norbert Samuelson, Temple University (Jewish Philosophy)
Jonathan Z. Smith, University of Chicago (Studia Philonica)

Number 161
PHILO'S JEWISH IDENTITY

by
Alan Mendelson

PHILO'S JEWISH IDENTITY

by
Alan Mendelson

Scholars Press
Atlanta, Georgia

PHILO'S JEWISH IDENTITY

© 1988
Brown University

Library of Congress Cataloging in Publication Data
Mendelson, Alan.
  Philo's Jewish identity.

  (Brown Judaic studies ; no. 161)
  1. Philo, of Alexandria. 2. Judaism--History--586
B.C.-210 A.D. 3. Judaism--Apologetic works--History and
criticism. I. Title. II. Series.
B689.Z7M46   1988   296.3'092'4   88-33719
ISBN 1-55540-307-7 (alk. paper)

Printed in the United States of America
on acid-free paper

For David and Daniel

CONTENTS

ACKNOWLEDGMENTS ix
ABBREVIATIONS xii

I. PERSPECTIVES ON JEWISH IDENTITY 1

    Philo's Inner World 2
    Philo's External World 15
    Fidelity to Ancestral Customs 22
    Accommodation 25

II. ORTHODOXY 29

    "God is and is from eternity" 31
    "He that really IS is One" 33
    "He has made the world" 38
    "He has made it one world..." 44
    "He ever exercises forethought" 46

III. ORTHOPRAXY 51

    Circumcision 54
    Sabbath 58
    Festivals, Sacrifice, and the Day
        of Atonement 62
    Dietary Laws 67
    Intermarriage 71

IV. PHILO'S APOLOGETIC 77

    Theoretical Interlude 77
    Indolence and the Sabbath 82
    Illicit Pleasures and Asceticism 86
    Misanthropy and Philanthropy 103

V.	DRAWING THE LINE		115
	A People Apart	115	
	Jewish Virtue; or, the Spiritual Supremacy of the Jews	128	

EPILOGUE by Ben F. Meyer   139

INDICES   143

ACKNOWLEDGMENTS

The idea for this work developed and was nurtured at McMaster University in an atmosphere of scholarly collaboration and good will. In 1976 the Canada Council (now the Social Sciences and Humanities Research Council of Canada) began funding a five-year research project at McMaster on Normative Self-Definition in Judaism and Christianity. I was fortunate to be part of this endeavor. As my contribution to the Project, I was to write a joint work with John J. Collins and David Winston on the topic of Jewish Self-Definition in the Greek-speaking Diaspora. This ambitious plan eventually evolved into three separate studies: John Collins' *Between Athens and Jerusalem: Jewish Identity in the Hellenistic Diaspora* (New York, 1983), David Winston's *The Mind of Philo of Alexandria* (forthcoming), and the present work. I am very grateful to my would-be co-authors, for over a long period of time they openly shared their ideas and exhibited every academic and personal virtue.

David Winston's relation to this study actually needs to be chronicled in more detail. Some years ago, I showed him the first draft of my work. His response was several pages of learned comments. I thought his remarks were so illuminating that I asked for, and happily received, permission to transcribe many of them as footnotes to this work. They are pleasant reminders of our collaborative efforts.

Over the years, I learned from many scholars who visited McMaster and contributed to seminars and symposia sponsored by the Project. The published record of the symposia appears in three volumes edited by E.P. Sanders and others under the general title of *Jewish and Christian Self-Definition* (London and Philadelphia, 1980-82). I would like to express my particular appreciation to four members of my Department: A.I. Baumgarten, Ben Meyer, Ed Sanders and Gérard Vallée. These colleagues gave of themselves to create a community of scholarship unique in my experience. Ben Meyer took collegiality one step further. He presented a paper at the 1987 meetings of the Learned Societies of Canada which contained some felicitous reflections on my work. He kindly allowed me to publish his thoughts as an epilogue, and I do so with gratitude.

I should like to thank other members of the McMaster community: Alan C. Frosst, Erin Phillips, and Cecile Spencer. Earle Hilgert, Burton Mack, and Barry Walfish also facilitated my work, and I am grateful to them.

Above all I would like to thank my wife Sara who stepped out of her studies of the seventeenth century long enough to comment with insight on my work. She remains my most trustworthy and perceptive critic.

In this book, I inquire into the minimum requirements for Jewish life in the Diaspora. The issues addressed here do not grow exclusively out of the thought of Philo of Alexandria. Indeed the same questions resonate through the ages. This book is dedicated to my children as they begin to assume their roles in the great chain of Jewish life.

23 December 1987
Hamilton, Ontario

PRINCIPAL ABBREVIATIONS

ANRW   *Aufstieg und Niedergang der römischen Welt*, ed. W. Haase. Berlin, 1979-87, II, vols. 19.1, 20.1, 20.2, 21.1, and 23.2.

Ant.   Josephus, *Antiquitates Judaicae*.

Apion. Josephus, *Contra Apionem*.

BAJ   J.J. Collins, *Between Athens and Jerusalem: Jewish Identity in the Hellenistic Diaspora*. New York, 1983.

BJ   Josephus, *Bellum Judaicum*.

CPJ   *Corpus papyrorum Judaicorum*, ed. V.A. Tcherikover, A. Fuks, and M. Stern. Cambridge, 1957-64. 3 vols.

GLA   M. Stern, *Greek and Latin Authors on Jews and Judaism*. Jerusalem, 1976-84. 3 vols.

JBL   *Journal of Biblical Literature*.

PLCL   *Philo Loeb Classical Library*, ed. G.H. Whitaker, F.H. Colson, and R. Marcus. London, 1929-53. 10 vols. and 2 supplementary vols.

SEPA   A. Mendelson, *Secular Education in Philo of Alexandria*. Cincinnati, 1982.

ABBREVIATIONS OF PHILO'S TREATISES

Abr.	*De Abrahamo*
Aet.	*De Aeternitate Mundi*
Agr.	*De Agricultura*
Cher.	*De Cherubim*
Conf.	*De Confusione Linguarum*
Congr.	*De Congressu Eruditionis Gratia*
Cont.	*De Vita Contemplativa*
Decal.	*De Decalogo*
Det.	*Quod Deterius Potiori Insidiari Soleat*
Deus	*Quod Deus Sit Immutabilis*
Ebr.	*De Ebrietate*
Flac.	*In Flaccum*
Fug.	*De Fuga et Inventione*
Gig.	*De Gigantibus*
Her.	*Quis Rerum Divinarum Heres Sit*
Hypoth.	*Hypothetica*
Jos.	*De Josepho*
LA	*Legum Allegoriarum*
Legat.	*Legatio ad Gaium*
Mig.	*De Migratione Abrahami*
Mos.	*De Vita Mosis*
Mut.	*De Mutatione Nominum*
Op.	*De Opificio Mundi*
Plant.	*De Plantatione*
Post.	*De Posteritate Caini*
Praem.	*De Praemiis et Poenis*
Prob.	*Quod Omnis Probus Liber Sit*
Prov.	*De Providentia*
QE	*Quaestiones et Solutiones in Exodum*
QG	*Quaestiones et Solutiones in Genesim*
Sacr.	*De Sacrificiis Abelis et Caini*
Somn.	*De Somniis*
Spec.	*De Specialibus Legibus*
Virt.	*De Virtutibus*

I. PERSPECTIVES ON JEWISH IDENTITY

Philo of Alexandria's geographical isolation from the mainstream of rabbinic Judaism makes him one of the most fascinating witnesses of Judaism in the post-biblical period. Since the needs of Alexandrian Jews differed from those of contemporary Jews living in Palestine, Philo presents us with a distinctive view of the Jewish faith. This book is an attempt to come to terms with the foundation of Philo's faith by asking how Philo conceived of his Jewish identity. This issue lies at the heart of Philo's religious sensibilities.

The problem of Philo's Jewish identity may be approached by asking two complementary questions. First, how did Philo regard himself as a Jew among the other nations? Secondly, how did Philo regard himself as a Jew among other Jews? The first question explores Philo's relationship to the external world; the second focusses on the inner society of Philo's co-religionists.

Another way of formulating this distinction is to characterize two aspects of Philo's life as a Jew.[1] On the one hand, as a distinguished member of a Jewish community which perceived itself under siege, Philo devoted considerable energy to defining, both in matters of belief and practice, the perimeters of the Jewish domain. From this perspective, Philo would have been concerned with a number of basic questions. How can we identify a man as

---

[1] A.L. Epstein has observed in *Ethos and Identity: Three Studies in Ethnicity* (London, 1978) that individuals often express their self-awareness within different frames of reference. "As members of society each of us carries simultaneously a range of identities just as each of us occupies a number of statuses and plays a variety of roles" (p. 100).

a Jew? What minimal set of beliefs and practices keeps a man within the Jewish fold? How should Jews relate to their gentile neighbors? In answering these questions, Philo takes his position on the bulwark, serving as an apologist to the pagan authorities and intelligentsia. He also acts as a spiritual guide for Jews who may have considered assimilation or accommodation to alien ways.

On the other hand, Philo was concerned with issues which had meaning primarily for a small circle within the Jewish community. The question for Philo now became, who is an ideal or proper Jew? The contrast here is not between Jew and gentile, but between Jews of different persuasions. Recognizing a man, minimally, as a fellow Jew is one thing; admitting him into your innermost religious councils is another. The lowest-common-denominator approach to Jewish identity is no longer sufficient. From this perspective, a certain amount of knowledge of, and sympathy with, Judaism is assumed. Instead of defining the perimeter, Philo devotes himself to the interior of the Jewish domain.

Philo's Inner World

Of the two perspectives outlined above, Philo's relations to the internal Jewish world are simpler. Consequently we shall deal with this aspect first. In *Somn.* 1.39 Philo distinguishes between "men of narrow citizenship" and "those who are on the roll of a greater country, even this whole world, men of higher thought and feeling."[2] From the context it is clear that both the "men of narrow citizenship" and their more cosmopolitan brethren are Jews. The bitter disagreement between them is based on differing approaches to the interpretations of Scripture. Indeed this one issue, more than any other, would have set Philo (and those sympathetic to him[3]) apart from his fellow Jews. Hermeneutic disagreements were not simply academic. For Philo, they were indicative of how the interpreter stood on such key questions as truth, tradition, and contemporary values. This is evident, for instance, in the following passage:

> Those to whose lot has fallen a generously gifted nature and a training blameless throughout...have truth for their fellow-traveller, and being admitted by her into the infallible mysteries of the Existent do not overlay the conception of God with any of the attributes of created being.... But they whose natural wit is more dense and dull, or whose early training has been mishandled, since they

---

[2]Unless otherwise noted, quotations of Philo in this book are taken from the Loeb Classical Library edition, transl. G.H. Whitaker, F.H. Colson, and R. Marcus (10 vols., 2 supplementary vols.; London, 1929-53).

[3]In this study, I am assuming that Philo was not unique in his approach to Judaism. Although it is impossible to determine how many Alexandrian Jews were sympathetic to him, there is every reason to regard Philo as *representative* of a school of biblical interpretation which had its beginnings earlier in the Hellenistic period and, by Philo's day, constituted a substantial presence in Alexandria. When I speak in this section of Philo's "group" or his "inner circle," I am referring to such like-minded individuals. For further thoughts on this subject, see B.L. Mack, "Philo and Exegetical Traditions in Alexandria," *ANRW* 21.1, pp. 242-43.

> have no power of clear vision, need physicians in the shape of admonishers, who will devise the treatment proper to their present condition.... All such may well learn the untruth, which will benefit them, if they cannot be brought to wisdom by truth (*Deus* 61-64).

We may distinguish here two sorts of Jews. First of all, there is Philo's group--presumably Jews who are capable of appreciating wisdom. The group with whom Philo does not identify needs the literal detail of Scripture. Incapable of grasping the higher truths of theology, these Jews live comfortably with anthropomorphic conceptions. Philo's attitude toward Jews of this complexion is a mixture of toleration and condescension.

It is not always necessary to expose simple Jewish believers to the truth as Philo himself saw it. An interesting elaboration of this point may be found in *Somn.* 1.233:

> ...an old saying is still current that the deity goes the round of the cities, in the likeness now of this man now of that man, taking note of wrongs and transgressions. The current story may not be a true one, but it is at all events good and profitable for us that it should be current.

Philo's cast of mind recalls that of the guardians in Plato's *Republic*. In the interest of harmony, the rulers of that ideal *polis* pressed pragmatic "truths" or lies-in-words upon the ordinary people (cf. *Rep.* 412d-415d). In both Philo and Plato, simple souls are encouraged to believe certain things which the elite would reject. Philo justifies this with a blatant appeal to social control: that is, he notes that some men conceive of a God who

> is displeased at wrongdoings, is inexorable in His anger, and in addition to all this has provided Himself with shafts and swords and all other instruments of vengeance against the unrighteous. For it is something to be thankful for if they can be taught self-control by the terror held over them by these means (*Somn.* 1. 236-37).

While Philo shows empathy for his dull brethren, he clearly sets himself apart from them. In this connection, we should notice the mystic terminology in *Deus* 61-64. For our purposes, it is immaterial whether Philo is referring to literal mysteries in that passage. At the very least, Philo uses the language of the mysteries to establish the exclusivity of his own circle. This is precisely the effect produced by *Cher.* 48 in which Philo tells the "initiated" (*mystai*) to receive certain thoughts "as holy mysteries" and to guard against revealing them to any of the profane or uninitiated (*amyētōn*).

Philo's stance vis-à-vis his fellow Jews could be described, in a word, as elitist. As he writes in an autobiographical digression, "So behold me daring, not only to read the sacred messages of Moses, but also in my love of knowledge to peer into each of them and unfold and reveal what is not known to the multitude" (*Spec.* 3.6). After discussing Isaac's name in *Mut.* 138, Philo states, "This saying is not for all to hear." Then he refers to a select few, men "whose ears are opened and pricked up to receive these holy words..." (*ibid.*).[4] These remarks, taken in conjunction with the passages cited in the previous paragraph, might suggest that Philo thought of himself as a repository of esoteric knowledge. We might conclude further that Philo, like some of his pagan contemporaries, endeavored to keep his knowledge from all but his closest associates. In fact, nothing could be further from the truth. Philo specifically rejects an esoteric model in *Spec.* 1.319. While remaining an elitist, Philo exhibits an openness which would allow any spiritually qualified man to join his inner circle. This would seem to be the point of his addressing the following rhetorical question to the mystics:

> For tell me, ye mystics, if these things are good and profitable, why do you shut yourselves up in profound darkness and reserve their benefits for three or four alone, when by producing them in the midst of the marketplace you might extend them to every man and thus enable all to share in security a better and happier life (*Spec.*1. 320)?

The implication here is that Philo himself (and those associated with him) upheld the opposite virtues. The realm of the spirit is neither a closed book nor a secret society. But those who are considered a part of it must necessarily accept certain principles of theology and biblical interpretation.

---

[4]Also see *Abr.* 147: "Such is the natural and obvious rendering of the story as suited for the multitude. We will proceed at once to the hidden and inward meaning which appeals to the few who study soul characteristics rather than bodily forms." Similar sentiments are expressed in *Abr.* 200 and 236.

As we have already seen, Philo's inner circle was particularly sensitive to the anthropomorphic depiction of God. While Philo is never enthusiastic about the practice of depicting the divine in human terms, at times he justifies it on pedagogical grounds. This is clear in *Conf.* 134-35:

> ...to suppose that the Diety approaches or departs, goes down or goes up, or in general remains stationary or puts Himself in motion, as particular living creatures do, is an impiety which may be said to transcend the bounds of ocean or of the universe itself. No, as I have often said elsewhere, the lawgiver is applying human terms to the superhuman God, to help us, his pupils, to learn our lesson.

At other times, he simply denounces the practice, expressing his opposition to those who "overlay the conception of God with... attributes of created being" (*Deus* 61). On the basis of this and related passages, we might be tempted to identify Philo and his associates by the rigor and purity of their theological language.

Yet, as Philo is forced to recognize, there are limits to the exercise: human understanding is too frail to grasp divine power.[5] Or, as Philo expresses the problem elsewhere, "we cannot get outside ourselves, but frame our conceptions of the Uncreated from our own experience" (*Conf.* 98). In the final analysis,

---

[5]Philo's question in *Deus* 78 is significant: "Can you think it possible that your understanding should be able to grasp in their unmixed purity those uncreated potencies, which stand around Him and flash forth light of surpassing splendour?" Also see *ibid*. 55 and *LA* 3.206 as well as D. Winston, *Philo of Alexandria: The Contemplative Life, the Giants, and Selections* in the series *Classics of Western Spirituality* (New York, 1981), pp. 22-24.

everyone uses the language of men in referring to God. Philo's closest associates may have been sophisticated, but essentially their language was not qualitatively different from that of the simple believer, and we cannot find here a key to their individuality.

What distinguished Philo's circle, then, was not so much the purity of their theological utterances as a keen awareness of two complementary beliefs: first, that the Bible was written on the level of the philosophically unsophisticated and, second, that the truth of Scripture could be approached, if not reached, by allegory. Both of these beliefs shaped the way in which Philo conceived of himself as a Jew. As a consequence of the first belief, Philo adopted a two-tiered conception of his co-religionists. As a consequence of the second, he committed himself to the propagation of an allegorical interpretation of Scripture. This last point deserves further attention, for we cannot assess Philo's place within the Jewish community without seeing in more detail how he found his way between the various schools of biblical interpretation which flourished in Alexandria.

Philo staked out his territory with care, taking issue with both literalists[6] and extreme allegorists. At times there are good reasons for avoiding the literal readings of the simple believer. As it stands, Scripture can be misleading; an example of this may be seen in *LA* 1.2:

> "And God finished on the sixth day His works which He had made" [Gen. 2:2]. It is quite

---

[6]See M.J. Shroyer, "Alexandrian Jewish Literalists," *JBL* 55 (1936), 261-84.

foolish to think that the world was created in six days or in a space of time at all.[7]

Scripture can also be obscure:

> "He" it continues, "that slayeth Cain shall loosen seven punishable objects" [Gen.4:15]. What meaning this conveys to those who interpret literally, I do not know.[8] For there is nothing to show what the seven objects are, nor how they are punishable, nor in what way they become loose and unstrung. We must make up our minds that all such language is figurative and involves deeper meanings (*Det.* 167).[9]

Finally, the Bible can be inconsistent. Having discussed Lev. 14:34-36 in *Deus* 131-132, Philo virtually throws up his hands:

> Now whether in the plain and literal sense of the ordinance these things are consistent with each other is a matter for those who are used to such questions and find pleasure in them. But *we* must say positively that no two things can be more consistent with each other than that ...(*Deus* 133).

At this point, Philo gives his allegorical interpretation (*ibid.* 134-35), which, it is interesting to note, turns the literal meaning on its head. A similar problem arises with biblical stories; for

---

[7] Philo regarded this passage as foolish because it was based on anthropomorphic misconceptions.

[8] Would Philo have made this statement if he had direct access to, and understanding of, the MT here?

[9] Another example of Philo retreating in the face of an obscure passage is *Plant.* 113.

instance, the literal account of the creation of woman appears to have strained the credulity:

> "And God brought a trance upon Adam, and he fell asleep; and He took one of his sides" and what follows [Gen. 2:21]. These words in their literal sense are of the nature of a myth (*to rhēton epi toutou mythōdes esti*).[10] For how could anyone admit that a woman, or a human being at all, came into existence out of a man's side (*LA* 2.19)?

As in the previous cases, Philo prefers to think of this passage allegorically (*ibid*. 21).

In spite of the examples given in the previous paragraph, Philo did not make it a practice of flying in the face of Scripture. Whenever possible, he retained the literal meaning of the biblical passage intact, adding an allegorical interpretation to the literal one, but not undermining it. Something of this order of priorities is evident in Philo's discussion of the confusion of languages at the Tower of Babel. Having given his own explanation, Philo refers to the interpretation of the literalists. Although he plainly did not share their views, he concedes:

> I would not censure such persons, for perhaps the truth is with them also. Still I would exhort them not to halt there, but to press on to allegorical interpretations and to recognize that the letter is to the oracle but as the shadow to the substance... (*Conf*. 190).

Philo deliberately contradicted Scripture only when the holy text itself (or its translation into Greek) raised patent difficulties

---

[10]Cf. *Agr*. 97.

for him as an exegete, theologian, or apologist. Especially in the latter role Philo felt called upon to defend Scripture against the attacks of unnamed parties who latched on to literal anomalies with a view to ridiculing Judaism.[11] He was very much aware of this problem, as the following passage indicates:

> Some of the quarrelsome and captious type of people who wish to attach blame where it is not due... and wage war to the death against what is holy, when they find anything which seems to them to fall short in propriety if taken literally, while really it is a symbol of the nature-truth which loves concealment, make no careful search for that truth, but disparage it and hold it up to obloquy (*Mut.* 60).

The views of one quarrelsome literalist and the divine retribution which was meted out to him are related in *Mut.* 61-62. This is an interesting episode because it implies that the critic had a rather detailed knowledge of biblical etymologies. Whether this attack came from a pagan or a lapsed Jew, Philo's response grows out of his concept of himself as one who transmitted allegorical truths to a heterogeneous Jewish population.

As we have seen, Philo was capable of avoiding the literal meaning of Scripture by escaping into allegory. What was his authority for so doing? The answer to this question lies in the

---

[11]Philo refers to the ridicule of critics in *Her.* 81. An atmosphere of contention is also evident in *Plant.* 70-72, *Somn.* 2.301, and *QG* 4.168. In the latter passage, Philo refers to the literalists in the opposition as uncultivated, lacking consistency of character and attributing "their own uneducatedness and stupidity and perversity and thoughtlessness to the holy Scriptures, which are more truthful than any other thing."

Bible itself, for in it Philo found various justifications for his exegetical methods. First of all, since Moses "is wont to use language and utter teachings larger and more daring than suit the ears of us feebler folk" (*Plant.* 62), some interpretation was always necessary. When a text was genuinely problematic, Scripture might point to a way out. For instance, in his opinion Gen. 37:14 all but gives the reader "a plain hint to avoid the literal interpretation" (*Det.* 15). Even more significant, Philo thought that the Bible itself allegorized. He found proof of this in the biblical description of the Garden of Eden in which "there are trees in no way resembling those with which we are familiar, but trees of Life, of Immortality, of Knowledge, of Apprehension, of Understanding, of the conception of good and evil." (*Plant.* 36). If Philo took these remarks (or others like them) as guidelines, he may have come to see his allegorical work as falling squarely within traditions of exegesis licensed by Moses.

Although Philo leaves some modern readers with the impression that he allegorized by free association,[12] Philo may not have perceived his own work in this light. The Bible for him did not contain a single superfluous word (*Fug.* 54)--an attitude which always brought Philo back to the text.[13] A good example of the esteem in which Philo held Scripture is *Somn.* 1.120:

---

[12] Cf. the remarks of L. H. Feldman in *Studies in Judaica: Scholarship on Philo and Josephus (1937-1962)* (New York, n.d.), p. 7.

[13] See *Conf.* 142-43. Here Philo finds it necessary to argue with scoffers who take Scripture to be redundant.

> Our admiration is extorted not only by the lawgiver's allegorical and philosophical teaching, but by the way in which the literal narrative inculcates the practice of toil and endurance.

Here Philo is so taken with the literal meaning of a passage that he places it on a par with the allegorical. Despite the free hand with which Philo seems to approach Scripture, he knew where to draw the line: he dissociated himself in no uncertain terms from those who allegorized the law without taking into account its literal prescriptions. Philo's own words are worth citing because they reveal the religious tensions within the Jewish community; they also indicate how Philo (and presumably his circle) resolved the issue of the letter and the spirit of the law:

> There are some who, regarding laws in their literal sense in the light of symbols of matters belonging to the intellect, are overpunctilious about the latter, while treating the former with easy-going neglect. Such men I for my part should blame for handling the matter in too easy and off-hand a manner: they ought to have given careful attention to both aims, to a more full and exact investigation of what is not seen and in what is seen to be stewards without reproach (*Mig.* 89).

Thus even as Philo soared on the wings of allegory, he was aware that he had to give the written word its due. His discussion of Exod. 22:27 shows the same concern:

> Let what has been said...suffice for the self-satisfied pedantic professors of literalism, and let us in accordance with the rules of allegory *tois allēgorias nomois*) make such remarks on this passage as are appropriate (*Somm.* 1.102).

The reference to rules in the passage just quoted is significant, for it suggests that, at least from Philo's point of view, allegorical material was not presented haphazardly. There seem to have been literary or religious conventions about such things: "Marvel not," says Philo, "if the sun, in accordance with the rules of allegory (*kata tous tēs allēgorias kanonas*), is likened to the Father and Ruler of the universe..." (*Somn.* 1.73).[14] What is more, there was some way of distinguishing between allegory done appropriately and that done inappropriately.

In the light of these observations, it is no wonder that a spirit of contention existed between different schools of biblical interpretation. Just such a spirit may be discerned in the following confrontation over the proper use of the word "season" (*kairos*) in LXX Num. 14:9:

> But they who say that season means the changes of the year strain the terms from their proper meaning, for they have not carefully studied the real natures of things but are deeply tainted with looseness of thought (*Mut.* 266).

Here Philo puts himself in opposition to other, presumably Jewish, interpreters. By drawing a distinction between himself and them, Philo not only is saying something about his opponents. He also is affirming that his own method reflects the true nature of reality.

Even though Philo distances himself from both literalists and extreme allegorists, he is hesitant to arrogate to himself the explicit label of "allegorist." For instance in *Abr.* 99 he remarks,

---

[14]Also see *Fug.* 108.

"I have also heard some natural philosophers (*physikōn andpōn*)[15] who took the passage allegorically, not without good reason. They said...." At this point Philo presents an allegorical interpretation without identifying himself with those who proposed it. There can be no doubt, however, that the allegory emanated from circles with which he was in deep sympathy.

Abr. 99 is not the only passage in which Philo fails to identify himself with those who allegorize. One might reasonably infer from this and similar passages (e.g. *Somn.* 1.118, *Jos.* 151, *Plant.* 35-36, and *Fug.* 179-81) that Philo's "failure" in this respect was deliberate. For in the final analysis Philo may not have regarded himself simply as a representative of one Alexandrian school among others. He may have thought of himself, instead, as a spokesman for the *true* interpretation of Scripture. The search for the truth could and often did lead Philo to allegory. But where circumstances dictated, Philo felt free to adopt other modes of explanation.[16]

Philo's External World

Although it is an over-simplification, we may think of Philo's pagan world as having two foci--Rome and Alexandria. Philo's legation to Rome brought him face to face with imperial power and prompted him, not for the first time in his life, to reflect on

---

[15] Cf. Colson's remarks in *PLCL* 6, 52-53, n.a.

[16] As we shall see in a later chapter, Philo was aware that allegory could lead to non-observance (cf. *Mig.* 89-93). Where the issue was crucial enough, as in the case of circumcision, Philo was wary about relying exclusively on allegorical explanations.

the plight of the Jews throughout the civilized world. In a sense, Rome called on Philo to be cosmopolitan, and it was in response to her that he wrote his two political treatises, *In Flaccum* and *Legatio ad Gaium*. Alexandria, on the other hand, represented a much more mundane, but vital struggle against the forces of intolerance, prejudice, and assimilation. If Rome brought out the cosmopolitan in Philo, Alexandria forced him to think more narrowly. The position of his family and his own learning, both secular and religious, enabled Philo to devote much of his life to the interpretation of Scripture. Whether he was a teacher with a lecture-hall full of questioning students or whether he was a closet philospher and pure exegete, Philo was responsive to the daily needs of the Jewish community of Alexandria.

We may begin with Philo's cosmopolitan concept of the Jewish commonwealth. That idea lies behind his treatment of Num. 33 in which Moses is confronted by tribes eager to separate from the children of Israel and settle in Trans-jordan. Philo appears to have seen in this situation a contemporary parallel, for he uses the occasion to remind his readers of the unity of the Jewish people. Those who wish to cross the Jordan, he says,

> have all equal rights with us; one race (*genos*), the same fathers, one house, the same customs, community of laws, and other things innumerable, each of which strengthens the tie of kinship and the harmony of goodwill (*Mos.* 1.324).

The Jewish world, as Philo conceived of it, extended from Rome to the Euphrates, from Macedonia to Libya (cf. *Legat.* 281-83). In short, owing to their populousness (*Flac.* 45-46), the Jews had spread throughout "the whole habitable world" (*oikoumenē, Legat.* 214).[17]

Despite ephemeral allegiances to countries of the dispersion, despite vast distances which separated Jewish "colonists" from their mother city, the focus of attention for Philo remained Jerusalem.[18] To that city the Jews, now scattered, would presumably be delivered "with one impulse ... guided in their pilgrimage by a vision divine and superhuman unseen by others but manifest to them as they pass from exile to their home" (*Praem.* 165). Although the exact meaning of these visionary words is elusive,[19] the position of Jerusalem and, more specifically, the Temple is clear. A Jew should be prepared to die to defend the sanctity of the Temple.[20] Even pagans were supposed to be aware of this--which is why Philo portrays Gaius as knowing that if the

---

[17] See the remarks on Jewish settlement by E.M. Smallwood in her edition of Philo's *Legatio ad Gaium* (Leiden, 1961), pp. 270-71 and 294-96.

[18] Y. Amir discusses the significance of the term *mētropolis* as applied to Jerusalem in "Philo's Version of the Pilgrimage to Jerusalem," *Perakim be-toldot Yerushalayim bi-yeme Bayit Sheni: sefer zikaron le-Avraham Shalit (Jerusalem in the Second Temple Period: Abraham Schalit Memorial Volume)*, ed. A. Oppenheimer, U. Rappaport, and M. Stern (Jerusalem, 1980), pp. 154f. This article has also appeared as "Die Wallfahrt nach Jerusalem in Philons Sicht" in a collection of essays by Amir, *Die hellenistische Gestalt des Judentums bei Philon von Alexandrien* (Neukirchen-Vluyn, 1983). Future references to this article will be to the Hebrew version: "Pilgrimage" (Heb.).

[19] Cf. Colson's note in *PLCL* 8, 418.

[20] Cf. *Deus* 17-18.

Temple were threatened the Jews would be willing to die "not once but a thousand times...rather than allow any of the prohibited actions to be committed" (*Legat.* 209). Nor were such expressions of loyalty adequate in themselves. Mosaic law does not ask men simply "to perform the rites in their houses, but bids them rise up from the ends of the earth and come to this temple" (*Spec.* 1.67-68). Temple-worship in one's own person is a measure of the worshipper's religious commitment. It obviously has an integral place in Philo's conception of Jewish identity (*ibid.* 69-75).[21]

Even though Jerusalem and the Temple played crucial roles in Philo's thought, in actual practice his attitudes were shaped by social and political realities. As Collins has remarked, "Attainment of rights in Alexandria is far higher on Philo's agenda than return to Jerusalem."[22] For example, Philo was well aware of the Biblical prescription in Deut. 16:16 which "enjoins that at three seasons of the year every male is to show himself before the Lord the God of Israel." Yet in his commentary on this verse (*LA* 3.11), Philo is more concerned to expatiate on the true (allegorical) meaning of "showing oneself" than he is to inform his co-religionists how to fulfill their traditional religious

---

[21]Cf. *Spec.* 1.71-78 and *Legat.* 156-157. Also see Collins, *BAJ*, pp. 116-17, and Amir, "Pilgrimage" (Heb.), p. 157.

[22]Collins, *BAJ*, p. 116.

obligations.[23] Philo's treatise on the sacrifices of Abel and Cain likewise contains no reference to the Jewish obligation to sacrifice in Jerusalem. In the same vein, Philo makes only one reference to a pilgrimage of his own (*Prov.* 2.64), and he does so in a fragment the authenticity of which has been questioned. Considerations of this sort lend credence to the view that Philo did not make pilgrimages to Jerusalem on a regular basis.

In keeping with his own distance from Temple-worship, Philo comments on the paradoxes of religious devotion: "It often happens that people who are actually in unconsecrated spots are really in most sacred ones" (*LA* 1.62). By the same token, pilgrims in Jerusalem might find themselves spiritually out of harmony with their surroundings. Since in some situations it is better not to make a pilgrimage to Jerusalem, Philo eagerly spiritualizes the entire matter:

> Now the city of God is called in the Hebrew Jerusalem and its name when translated is "vision of peace." Therefore do not seek for the city of the Existent among the regions of the

---

[23]See S. Safrai, *Aliyah le-regel bi-yeme ha-Bayit ha-sheni (Pilgrimage at the Time of the Second Temple)* (Tel Aviv, 1965), Ch.2. (German edition: *Die Wallfahrt im Zeitalter des Zweiten Tempels* [Neukirchen-Vluyn, 1981].) Safrai makes several points relevant to the issue of Alexandrian pilgrimage to Jerusalem. First, there was an Alexandrian synagogue in Jerusalem (*Aliyah*, p. 56). Second, there were Alexandrian craftsmen in the city as well (*ibid.* p. 60). On the basis of this evidence, Safrai concludes that there was a significant Alexandrian Jewish presence in Jerusalem. Yet both Josephus and the Talmud indicate that pilgrimage, as a religious obligation, applied only to Jews living in Erez Yisrael itself (*ibid.* p. 43). Philo's apparent lack of concern with the issue of pilgrimage to Jerusalem is consistent with the voluntary nature of pilgrimage from the Diaspora.

> earth, since it is not wrought of wood or stone, but in a soul, in which there is no warring, whose sight is keen, which has set before it as its aim to live in contemplation and peace (*Somn.* 2.250).[24]

Philo's etymology allows him to argue that since God alone is true peace, the true Jerusalem is, at least in part, a state of the soul. This sentiment is repeated in *Cher.* 99-100:

> What house shall be prepared for God the King of kings, the Lord of all...? Shall it be of stone or timber? Away with the thought, the very words are blasphemy. For though the whole earth should suddenly turn into gold, or something more precious than gold...yet there would be no place where His feet could tread. One worthy house there is--the soul that is fitted to receive Him.

In these two passages, one senses the dilemma of the Alexandrian Jew who cannot abandon an institution which is at the core of his faith. At the same time, he may find it difficult, if not impossible, to observe the literal letter of the law (Deut. 16:16). Does this mean that Philo abandons the Law? The answer, as Philo explains in *De Migratione*, is negative:

> It is true... that the Feast[25] is a symbol of gladness of soul and of thankfulness to God, but we should not for this reason turn our backs on the general gatherings of the year's

---

[24]Cf. comments by Amir, "Pilgrimage" (Heb.), p. 158, and V. Nikiprowetzky, "La spiritualisation des sacrifices et le culte sacrificiel au Temple de Jérusalem chez Philon d'Alexandrie," *Semitica* 17 (1967), 97-116.

[25]Colson's note *b* in *PLCL* 4, 184: Or "keeping of festivals (in general)."

> seasons.... Why, we shall be ignoring the sanctity of the Temple and a thousand other things, if we are going to pay heed to nothing except what is shewn us by the inner meaning of things. Nay, we should look on all these outward observances as resembling the body, and their inner meanings as resembling the soul (*Mig.* 92-93).

In Philo's treatment of the Temple, we can discern two conflicting themes--an idealistic allegiance to tradition and a realistic accommodation to the exigencies of life. This conflict appears and reappears in other guises in Philo's works. Caught between two worlds, Philo took it as his mission to address the most vexing issues of his time. It is as if he deliberately placed himself on the bulwark, countering the successive claims of tradition, faith, reason, and practicality. A passage from *De Sacrificiis* illustrates, in general terms, how Philo perceived these opposing claims and how he sought to balance them:

> We must not indeed reject any learning that has grown grey through time, nay, we should make it our aim to read the writings of the sages and listen to proverbs and old-world stories from the lips of those who know antiquity.... Yet when God causes the young shoots of self-inspired wisdom to spring up within the soul, the knowledge that comes from teaching must straightway be abolished and swept off (*Sacr.* 79).

Since fidelity to ancestral custom and accommodation to reality have something of the status of first principles in Philo, we shall now consider them in more detail.

Fidelity to Ancestral Customs

Faithfulness to tradition was for Philo one key to survival in an alien environment. This may be illustrated by studying the contrasts in Philo's lives of Moses and Joseph. In Egypt, Moses was regarded as the son of the King's daughter. How easy it would have been for Moses to look down on his "relations and friends and set at naught the laws under which they were born and bred, and subvert the ancestral customs...by adopting different modes of life, and...lose all memory of the past" (*Mos.* 1.31). Instead, Moses was "zealous for the discipline and culture of his kinsmen and ancestors" (*ibid.* 32). Having adopted the best of pagan culture (*ibid.* 21-24), he remained true to his heritage.[26]

Philo's Joseph, unlike his Moses, is an ambiguous character.[27] Joseph "is quite properly said to assume a coat of varied colours, for political life is a thing varied and multiple, liable to innumerable changes brought about by personalities, circumstances, motives..." (*Jos.* 32). From Philo, a staunch believer in the immutability of the truth, this sketch of Joseph is unflattering. Yet Philo is careful to say that Joseph, despite his faults in character, "strongly disapproved" of neglecting the customs of the Hebrews (*ibid.* 202-203). Later, in the same treatise, Jacob expresses his fears about the alien customs to which the young were exposed in Egypt:

> For he knew how natural it is for youth to lose
> its footing and what licence to sin belongs to

---

[26] Mendelson, *SEPA*, pp. 63f.

[27] Cf. E.R. Goodenough, *The Politics of Philo Judaeus: Practice and Theory* (New Haven, 1938), Ch.3.

> the stranger's life, particularly in Egypt where things created and mortal are deified, and in consequence the land is blind to the true God. He knew what assaults wealth and renown make on minds of little sense, and that left to himself, since his father's house supplied no monitor to share his journey, alone and cut off from good teaching, he would be readily influenced to change to alien ways (*ibid.* 254).

Jacob's concern about assimilation is particularly poignant because there is no biblical parallel to the passage. Philo attributes these thoughts to a patriarch; in fact they belong to Philo himself.

The situation of both Moses and Joseph touched Philo directly. Both biblical characters found political power within reach. To Philo, who saw these stories in contemporary terms, this meant that the temptation to assimilate in each case was great. Although Joseph seems to have taken advantage of the situation more than Moses did, neither one allowed himself to abandon the ancient customs of his people. The importance to Philo of adhering to ancestral ways is underscored by the far-fetched quality of the following interpretation:

> Another commandment of general value is "Thou shalt not remove thy neighbour's landmarks which thy forerunners have set up" [Deut. 19:14]. Now this law...applies not merely to allotments and boundaries of land in order to eliminate covetousness but also to the safeguarding of ancient customs. For customs are unwritten laws, the decisions approved by men of old, not inscribed on monuments nor on leaves of paper which the moth destroys, but

on the souls of those who are partners in the same citizenship (*Spec.* 4.149).[28]

To Philo, those Jews who treat the laws in a cavalier fashion misconstrue their true intention. What is more, in acting "as though they were living alone by themselves in a wilderness" (*Mig.* 90), they violate the social ethic of the Jews. Fidelity to ancient custom is, above all, a social concern. This is illustrated in Philo's formulation of the crime and punishment of Onan. Having stated that Onan received his just dessert, Philo elaborates on the nature of his transgression:

> ...if there shall be any whose every deed is self-seeking, who have no regard for the honouring of their parents, for the ordering of their children aright, for the safety of their country, for the maintenance of the laws, for the security of good customs, for the better conduct of things private and public, for the sanctity of temples, for piety towards God, miserable shall be their fate. To sacrifice life itself for any single one of these that I have named is honour and glory (*Deus* 17-18).

Clearly Onan represents the victory of self-love over the needs of the community; he epitomizes the private individual's repudiation of all social values. His death is warranted because his life undermines those elements of ancestral custom and community cohesiveness which Philo held most dear. From these reflections, Philo takes the next logical step: there comes a point when a Jew must be willing to sacrifice himself to preserve his Jewish

---

[28]Cf. S. Sandmel, *Philo's Place in Judaism: A Study of Conceptions of Abraham in Jewish Literature* (New York, 1971), pp. 18f.

Perspectives on Jewish Identity 25

identity. In this monograph an attempt will be made to determine where some of these points are.

Accommodation

Philo's desire to remain true to the customs of his ancestors co-exists in an uneasy truce with a need to accommodate himself to the social and religious realities of his environment. To illustrate Philo's adaptability, we may examine his treatment of the biblical injunction "Whosoever curseth his God (*Anthrōpos, hos ean katarasētai theon*) shall bear his sin. And he that blasphemeth the name of the Lord shall surely be put to death" (LXX Lev. 24:15-16).[29] Now despite the parallelism of these two verses which would seem to suggest that the Israelite God is being referred to in the first verse--despite the use of the singular *theon* in the LXX which would point to the same conclusion--Philo emphatically denies the identification of *theon* with the Jewish deity:

> ...clearly by "god" he [Moses] is not here alluding to the Primal God, the Begetter of the Universe, but to the gods of the different cities who are falsely so called, being fashioned by the skill of painters and sculptors. For the world as we know it is full of idols of wood and stone, and suchlike images. We must refrain from speaking insultingly of these, lest any of Moses' disciples get into the habit of

---

[29]D. Winston, in a private communication, notes: "See Z. Frankel, *Ueber den Einfluss der palästinischen Exegese auf die alexandrinische Hermeneutik* (Leipzig, 1851), pp. 130-31. Cf. Josephus, *Ant.* 4.207; *Apion.* 2.237. Philo's interpretation depends on the LXX."

treating lightly the name "god" in general... (*Mos.* 2.205).[30]

The purpose of Lev. 24:15-16, according to Philo's interpretation, is to prevent Jews from cursing pagan *gods*. But why should Philo, who disparages pagan deities at every turn in his writings, be so concerned about Jewish deference toward "idols of wood and stone?"[31] The answer to this question lies in the experience of the Diaspora Jew for whom it was axiomatic that one should refrain from any public act which might bring Jewry into disrepute. If one does behave with proper restraint, then, as Philo points out in a related passage, "the truly certain and existent (God) may be well spoken of and praised in the mouths of all" (*QE* 2.5).[32] In this way, the glory of the God of Israel is manifested to the nations. At the same time, those who worshipped the God of Israel could expect, or at least hope for, an improvement in the way they were treated.

How a Jew should relate to pagan gods in his environment is a particular problem. In its more generalized form, the problem becomes how a Jew should relate to the entire world of alien convention, custom, and law. Philo offers his solution in *De Ebrietate*, using the allegorical figures of the father and mother.

---

[30] Cf. E.R. Goodenough, *By Light, Light* (New Haven, 1935), p. 257.

[31] Cf. D. Flusser, "Paganism in Palestine" in *The Jewish People in the First Century*, ed. S. Safrai *et al.* (Philadelphia, 1976), Vol. 2, p. 1097.

[32] This is part of Philo's commentary on LXX Exod.22:28a (=MT Exod.22:27a). Also see *Spec.* 1.53.

"The father is reason, masculine, perfect, right reason" (*ton arrena kai teleion kai orthon logon*); the mother is secular education (*enkyklion...paideian, Ebr.* 33).³³

> Education, the mother, bids us give ear to rules laid down by human ordinance, rules which have been made in different cities and countries and nations by those who first embraced the apparent in preference to the true (*Ebr.* 34).

Elsewhere Philo says that the mother "enacts from city to city the ordinances which custom and opinion approve, her legislation differing with the different peoples" (*Ebr.* 64). The dichotomy which Philo establishes here is between God-given laws of Israel as found in the Torah and the ordinary human laws of the nations. The Torah, in harmony with reason, reflects the true nature of reality. The laws of the different cities, however, are chaotic when considered collectively and insubstantial when compared to the Torah.³⁴

The allegory of the father and mother allows for various alternatives: a man might obey one parent, both, or neither. The option which Philo fears most is represented by the man who obeys only his mother. Recognizing nothing but the authority of local custom and law, this man flies in the face of received tradition and truth. Philo regards him as an anathema:

> [He] bows down to the opinions of the multitude and undergoes all manner of transformations in conformity with the ever-varying aspirations of human-life, like the

---

³³See Mendelson, *SEPA*, pp. 45-46, and *Ebr.* 55.

³⁴Cf. *Ebr.* 193-94 and remarks in Goodenough, *Politics*, p. 81.

> Egyptian Proteus.... He plays the demagogue, and the laws which he lays down contradict the laws of nature; for his eyes are fixed on semblance... (*Ebr.* 36-37).

Yet despite this harsh judgment, local custom and law are never actually repudiated. Instead, Philo incorporates them into a two-part ideal. Those who obey both parents, Philo says, are "valiant guardians of the laws... and faithful stewards of the customs.... Their father, right reason, has taught them to honour the Father of the all; their mother, instruction, has taught them not to make light of those principles which are laid down by convention and accepted everywhere" (*Ebr.* 80-81). This is the reasoning of a man who has made his peace, possibly after a long struggle, with harsh realities.[35]

Behind Philo's efforts to accommodate himself to the outside world lies a perception that he is a member of a religious minority. In cities throughout the inhabited world, Jewish communities were vulnerable; the whims of local denizens and distant rulers could always upset the balance (*Legat.* 371). Philo's awareness of the Jews' precarious existence and his willingness to adapt because of it are two starting points in our study.

---

[35]On Alexandrian Jewish adjustment of biblical rules see B. Wardy, "Philo and the Haggada as Treated in Modern Scholarship, 1875-1975" (unpublished Ph.D. dissertation, McGill University, 1981), pp. 192-95.

II. ORTHODOXY

At the conclusion of *De Opificio Mundi*, Philo lists five principles or articles of religious belief. Modern commentators seem to agree that these principles constitute a central part of Philo's faith. Goodenough, for instance, declared that this was "the first creed of history."[1] In the present chapter, I shall take this assessment one step further: these articles are keys to Philo's concept of orthodoxy. A Jew who embraced these principles (and the inferences drawn from them) would be well on his way toward doctrinal correctness within Philonic Judaism. By the same token, Philo would have regarded anyone who failed to believe them as belonging to an alien faith.[2] These articles, then, are a kind of touchstone, a lowest common denominator of religious belief, which Philo would have regarded as essential for the preservation of Jewish identity.

Philo gives the creed in two forms. The first formulation (*Op.* 170 to the beginning of *Op.* 172) contains brief explanations. The second (*Op.* 172) appears to be a summary and is given here, for convenience, as a list:

[1] God is and is from eternity...

[2] He that really IS is One...

[3] He has made the world...

---

[1] E.R. Goodenough, *An Introduction to Philo Judaeus* (second ed; Oxford, 1962), p. 37. Elsewhere Goodenough calls this passage "the starting point of what is to Philo the Jewish life" (*Light*, p. 122). Also see H.A. Wolfson, *Philo* (2 vols.; Cambridge, 1947), I, 164.

[2] Those who build the tower of Babel in *Conf.* 114 seem to abrogate the creed.

[4] [He] has made it one world, unique as Himself is unique...

[5] He ever exercises forethought for His creation... .

At the outset, we should stress that these propositions are not only theological or philosophical in nature. They also have a social dimension and are firmly rooted in Philo's experience of contemporary Jewish life. Thus it would be an oversimplification to say that the first principle is simply an abstract belief in the existence of God and the second is an assertion of monotheism, *etc*. Philo's awareness of himself as a Jew was not wholly abstract. Indeed, upon inspection, each element of the creed reveals two aspects: that is, a positive, inner perception which describes some common attribute belonging to the Jews as a group and, then, a negative formulation which looks without and sets the group apart from others.[3]

In this light, we may consider the first principle: "God is and is from eternity...". Here Philo is not simply asserting that the Jews are monotheists. He is asserting that the Jews are not polytheists--that *they* (the non-Jews) are polytheists. Part of the richness of Philo's creed is that each article has (explicitly or implicitly) a dual aspect. In the analysis which follows, we shall try to discuss both sides of the coin.

---

[3] In this paragraph I rely on Epstein's concept of ethnic identity as presented in *Ethos and Identity*, pp. 100-102. Also see J.Z. Smith, *Map is not Territory: Studies in the History of Religion* (Leiden, 1978), pp. 241-42.

(1) *"God is and is from eternity"*

The first article both affirms the existence of God and posits that existence from eternity. Needless to say, this article is a *sine qua non* for Jewish life. It is very unlikely that Philo could conceive of a community which called itself Jewish and yet did not subscribe to this principle. The same would apply to any individual within that community. The existence of God is so central to Philo's conception of Judaism that further elaboration is unnecessary. Yet one brief passage may be seen as epitomizing the issue for Philo. In Exod. 3:13, Moses asks God how he (Moses) is to respond when asked a question about the divine name. For the children of Israel, who were being molded into a nation, this was *the* crucial question. To know the name of one's God is to learn something about his nature. At the same time, it is a way of establishing a primary fact about one's own identity. Philo appreciated that the issue was a turning point for the children of Israel. He also saw God's answer (in Exod. 3:14) as crucial for the philosophical understanding of God by his own contemporaries.

Philo's interpretation of Exod. 3:14 (LXX: *Egō eimi ho ōn*) is given in a number of different passages.[4] In *Mos.* 1.75, for instance, God says to Moses:

> First tell them that I am He Who IS, that they may learn the difference between what IS and what is not, and also the further lesson that no name at all can properly be used of Me, to whom alone existence belongs.

---

[4]In addition to *Mos.* 1.75, quoted here, see *Mut.* 11, *Somn.* 1.231, and *Det.* 160-162.

In reply to a question about his name, then, God asserts his existence. In this way, Philo points to a basic truth about God's being. This truth is enshrined in the first article of Philo's creed.

Philo's awareness of the nature of Judaism led him to postulate the existence and eternity of God. But his awareness of the external world induced him to add that the first article of the creed was written

> with a view to atheists, some of whom have hesitated and have been of two minds about His eternal existence, while the bolder sort have carried their audacity to the point of declaring that the Deity does not exist at all...(*Op.* 170).

A concern with atheism is the other side of the coin and lies behind Philo's formulations of God's existence. Philo keeps returning to the idea of atheism, and he stresses it even if he must take certain liberties with Scripture. For an example, Lev. 24:10-16 relates the story of a man who blasphemed against God. In Philo's rendition, the emphasis shifts to reflect Alexandrian Jewish concerns. The man still curses, but Philo stresses his connections with Egyptian impiety and atheism:[5]

> A certain base-born man...his father an Egyptian, his mother a Jewess, had set at naught the ancestral customs of his mother and turned aside, as we are told, to the impiety of Egypt and embraced the atheism of that people. For the Egyptians almost alone among the nations have set up earth as a power to challenge heaven (*Mos.* 2. 193-194).

---

[5] In the biblical account, the man is said to be the son of an Israelite woman and an Egyptian father, but nothing is said of his atheism. Cf. Wolfson, *Philo*, I, 165-67.

Later in the same treatise, Philo reiterates the point: the man was "urged by fondness for Egyptian atheism" (*ibid.* 196). Denunciations of atheism appear elsewhere in the Philonic corpus. In *Mig.* 69, for instance, atheism is linked with polytheism and is called a doctrine which is antagonistic to the soul; as Philo says, "The Law has expelled both of these doctrines from the sacred assembly." In the eyes of the Jewish community, then, atheism goes beyond the limits of toleration and the atheist has no place in society. To formulate this in a more positive way, belief in the existence of God is required in order to maintain one's membership in the community.

(2) *"He that really IS is One"*

The affirmation of monotheism is the second article of Philo's creed.[6] Philo is explicit once again about the external target of his words, for he tells us that this article is formulated "with a view to the propounders of polytheism, who do not blush to transfer from earth to heaven mob-rule, that worst of evil polities" (*Op.* 170). As *Mig.* 69 indicates, polytheists must be expelled from the assembly. A passage from *De Specialibus Legibus* expresses the same sentiments, but gives a more detailed account of how the community regards the polytheist:

---

[6]For Philo's reflections on God's oneness, see *LA* 1.51-52 and 2.1-3. Philo was not alone in identifying Judaism by its monotheism. Tacitus commented on it (*Hist.* 5.5.4), and Philo depicted the Emperor Gaius as being aware that the Jews' belief in God precluded loyalty to any other deity (such as himself). See *Legat.* 115-18, 162-64, and 353.

> If anyone cloaking himself under the name and guise of a prophet and claiming to be possessed by inspiration lead us on to the worship of the gods recognized in the different cities, we ought not listen to him and be deceived by the name of prophet. For such a one is no prophet, but an impostor.... And if... anyone else who seems to be kindly disposed, urge us to a like course, bidding us fraternize with the multitude, resort to their temples, and join in their libations and sacrifices, we must punish him as a public and general enemy, taking little thought for the ties which bind us to him...(*Spec.* 1.315-16).

Philo concludes his discussion by stating that "lovers of piety" will "deem it a religious duty to seek his death" (*ibid.*). The severity of the punishment for polytheism is a measure of the threat it posed not only to the biblical Israelites, but to Philo's own Alexandrian contemporaries.[7]

It is important to emphasize at this point that Philo did not treat all forms of polytheism in the same fashion. In *Decal.* 52-81, Philo's general discussion of the First Commandment, a distinct hierarchy emerges. Philo orders the world of alien worship in descending order from the more sublime to the ridiculous: astral worship, deification of the entire universe (pantheism), deification of certain elements within the universe, idol worship, worship of domesticated animals, and finally worship

---

[7]Likewise, in *Spec.* 1.54-55, Philo says that "if any members of the nation betray the honour due to the One they should suffer the utmost penalties." The example given (*ibid.* 56-57) follows Num. 25; in it polytheistic practices are punished by death.

of savage animals.[8] Philo is particularly restrained in his criticism of astral worshippers (*Decal.* 64). He disagrees with their fundamental assumption "that the world was not God's work, but itself God" (*Heres* 97). Nevertheless, he uses neither sarcasm nor invective in stating his opposition. One possible reason for Philo's restraint lies in the "divine" status of the stars themselves.[9] Another is that according to Philo, the patriarch Abraham, who is a model for proselytes, actually spent his formative years as an astral worshipper.[10] Because the path from astral worship to wisdom was a respectable one to take, Philo did not want to obstruct it with strong objections.

Philo's treatment of those who deify either the entire universe or part of it is also moderate. Philo criticizes them for "magnifying the subjects above the ruler" (*Decal.* 66), but he states in the same breath that their offense is less than those who worship the works of human hands. The pantheists to whom Philo refers here may very well have been contemporary Stoics.[11] Although Philo disagreed with them on many issues, he was nevertheless influenced by their thought, and his restraint in

---

[8]Winston, in a private communication, notes: "Cf. Wisdom 13-15 for the presentation of three forms of idolatry in the form of a *klimaks*." Winston's own edition of the Wisdom of Solomon prepared for the Anchor Bible (New York, 1979) gives an exemplary discussion of idolatry, pp. 247-91.

[9]Cf. Mendelson, *SEPA*, pp. 18ff.

[10]*Ibid.* pp. 20-21, 65, and 106, n. 94.

[11]Cf. Wolfson, *Philo*, I, 176-78.

discussing them is not surprising. The full force of Philo's invective is reserved for the Egyptians who worship wild beasts:

> ...anyone who knows the flavour of right instruction, horrified at this veneration of things so much the reverse of venerable, pities those who render it and regards them with good reason as more miserable than the creatures they honour...(*Decal.* 80).

It is a telling reflection on life in a pagan environment that Philo should consider it worth his while to distinguish between varieties of polytheistic experience. After all, to a monotheist all forms of polytheism might appear the same.[12] Philo's distinctions, however, are not the product of abstract theology, but rather a practical response to living "among the nations."

In Philo's treatment of polytheism we may discern direct correlations between the type of polytheism, the rank which Philo gives it, and the social or cultural niche which the polytheist himself would occupy in Alexandrian society. The first three groups in the hierarchy reveal some connection, however tenuous,

---

[12]Winston, in a private communication, notes that even the rabbis made distinctions between different varieties of pagan worship. Winston continues: "See S. Lieberman, *Hellenism in Jewish Palestine* (second ed.; New York, 1962), p. 130, n. 8. Cf. Wisdom 13:6. Moreover, Philo does not hesitate to use expressions which could mislead one into deifying the heavenly bodies (*Op.* 27; *Spec.* 1.19-20)....Clement of Alexandria was later prepared to accept the view (cf. Deut. 4:19) that the cult of the stars and planets may have been providentially allowed to heathen races as a stage in their emancipation from idolatry (Strom. 6.110.3; cf. Origen, *Comm. in Joh.* 2.3)."

with hellenistic thought.[13] Adherents to these groups may very well have included star-gazers who saw God in the movement of the celestial spheres, Stoics who perceived God everywhere, or the spirtual heirs of the pre-Socratic philosophers who discerned God in the oppositions of nature. What they had in common, an allegiance to the legacy of Greece, would have made them particularly attractive to Philo. None of them lived in a monotheistic world, but Philo seems to have thought that none was very distant from it.

This is all a far cry from the last three groups in the hierarchy. In Philo's view, those who worship idols or animals lack philosophical sophistication. Philo could only condemn their crude animism. Interestingly enough, Philo's cultural bias coincides with a social bias. The first three polytheistic beliefs would have been held by upper-class inhabitants of Alexandria, while the last three would have been held by Egyptians whom Philo found every occasion to ridicule. Both Greeks and Romans saw the Egyptians as socially inferior, so it is no wonder that Philo should have depicted their brand of polytheism in the worst possible light. Indeed, the vehemence of Philo's attack corresponds directly to his assessment of the social class of the particular polytheist concerned.

One of Philo's more intriguing objections to polytheism deserves mention here. In *Ebr.* 110, Philo states that "polytheism creates atheism in the souls of the foolish."[14] Philo seems to be

---

[13]Cf. Winston, *Selections*, pp. 307-308, n. 50.

[14]Also see *Praem.* 162 where the same sentiment is repeated.

saying that polytheism forces so may gods into the minds of the unwary that the total effect is one of confused disbelief. This process is reminiscent of a passage in Plato's *Euthyphro* (5d-9b).[15] But a more relevant parallel may be found in *De Ebrietate* itself.[16] In that treatise, there is a moment of epistemological crisis when the mind is so overwhelmed by conflicting perceptions and opinions that the process of knowledge comes to a standstill.[17] Polytheism, which intrudes on the spirit in much the same way, creates a similar crisis. One way for the foolish to resolve this uncomfortable state of mind is to adopt atheism.

(3) *"He has made the world"*

Philo now turns his attention to the creation of the world:[18]

> Thirdly, as I have said already, that the world came into being (*genētos ho kosmos*). This

---

[15] Also see Plato's *Republic* 365a-366a, 378 a-e.

[16] *Ebr.* 166-70, 199-205.

[17] Cf. Mendelson, *SEPA*, pp. 69-72 and Winston, *Selections*, p. 353, n. 257.

[18] I shall not discuss here the problematic issue of whether Philo believed in creation at a certain moment in time or eternal creation. In at least one passage, Philo appears to avoid this issue himself; in *Aet.* 14-15, he deliberately cuts short a technical discussion of what Plato meant by "the world as created." Instead, Philo stresses the creative functions of God by referring to the various names given to him by Plato. Cf. Winston, *Selections*, pp. 13-20, and D.T. Runia, *Philo of Alexandria and the Timaeus of Plato* (2 vols.; Free University of Amsterdam diss., 1983), I, 120-27.

> because of those who think that it is without beginning and eternal (*agenēton kai aidion*),[19] who thus assign to God no superiority at all (*Op.* 171).

When Philo affirms that the world came into being, he is stating in philosophical language a lesson he learned from the first verses of Genesis. The positive side of the coin thus seems relatively simple and straightforward. Only when we examine the opposition to this article does it become clear that Philo's concerns are more complex.

In order to appreciate the intricacies of Philo's position, we should examine a parallel passage. Here Philo uses the same words to describe the opposing view:

> There are some people who, having the world in admiration rather than the Maker of the world, pronounce it to be without beginning and everlasting (*agenēton te kai aidion*)[20] while with impious falsehood they postulate in God a vast inactivity; whereas we ought on the contrary to be astonied at His powers as Maker and Father, and not to assign to the world a disproportionate majesty (*Op.* 7).

In both *Op.* 171 and 7, *others* claim that the world is without beginning (or uncreated) and eternal. By maintaining that the world is not a work of creation--by asserting, furthermore, that the world is eternal and not subject to destruction--the opponents of the third article accomplish two things: first, they diminish the demiurgic power and grandeur of God and, second,

---

[19]Winston, *Selections*, p. 105: "uncreated and eternal."

[20]*Ibid.* p. 96: "uncreated and eternal."

they improperly raise the status of the world. Philo's main concern is to combat these unorthodox views.

Interestingly enough, an important passage in Philo's treatise on the eternity of the world points in the same direction. In *Aet.* 7, Philo sums up the problem in this way:

> Three views have been put forward on the question before us. [1] Some assert that the world is eternal (*aidion*), uncreated and imperishable (*agenēton te kai anōlethron*). [2] Some on the contrary say that it is created and destructible. [3] Others draw from both these. From the latter they take the idea of the created, from the former that of the indestructible and so have laid down a composite doctrine to the effect that the world is created and indestructible (*genēton kai aphtharton, Aet.* 7).

If we read further in this treatise, it becomes clear that Philo identifies himself with the third option. That is, in the passage *Aet.* 8-19, there is a discussion of the opinions of various Greek thinkers concerning the origin and ultimate destiny of the world. Hesiod, for instance, "very clearly states the view that the world is created." But, according to Philo, Moses has the last word because "long before Hesiod Moses the lawgiver of the Jews said in the Holy Books that it [the world] was created and imperishable" (*ibid.* 18-19). This reference to the authority of Moses leaves no doubt which option Philo prefers. To make his position even more clear Philo then quotes LXX Gen. 1:2 and 8:22 (*Aet.* 19).

We should now return to *Aet.* 7 and consider the first option mentioned by Philo. Obviously it is very similar to the unorthodox position described in *Op.* 171 and 7. The point on which [1] and [3] differ most is the creation of the world. As we saw in *De Opificio Mundi*, *they* deny creation; Philo, following Genesis, affirms it. And yet, what is actually at stake here is not only the question of creation. Aristotle, for instance, did not believe in the creation of the world.[21] Nevertheless, Philo praises him for showing "a pious and religious spirit" because he

> denounced the shocking atheism of those who stated ... that there was no difference between handmade idols and that great visible God who embraces the sun and moon and the pantheon... of the fixed and wandering stars (*Aet.* 10).

In other words, Philo has made his peace with those who assert that the world is without beginning *provided* that they are not atheists. What goes beyond the limits of Philo's toleration is to posit a principle which replaces God as the highest creative (or most active) principle in the world. Such an atheistic position, which we also see in Philo's depiction of the opponents to the third article in *Op.* 171 and 7, earns Philo's unremitting hostility. The main issue, then, is not creation *per se*, but the denial of a God whose very nature is to act:

> For God never leaves off making, but even as it is the property of fire to burn and of snow to chill, so it is the property of God to make: nay more so by far, inasmuch as He is to all besides the source of action (*LA* 1.5).

---

[21]On Aristotle's disagreement with those who "explained creation or reality without a moving Cause," see Goodenough, *Light*, p. 122, n. 2. (Goodenough cites *Metaphysics* 984a ff.) Also see Wolfson, *Philo*, I, 295-97.

A similar point may be made with regard to the ultimate destiny of the world. Philo's own position, as seen in *Aet.* 7, is that the world is indestructible (*aphtharton*). As for those who oppose the third article of the creed, Philo attributes to them the view that the world is eternal (*aidion*, *Op.* 171 and 7). In both cases, the world is thought to endure. Why does Philo take issue with a view which seems to approximate his own? Again the dispute concerns the nature of God.

The material world, in Philo's opinion, is friable. Echoing Plato, Philo claims: "... the world has become what it is, and its becoming (*genesis*) is the beginning of its destruction..." (*Decal.* 58). Left to its own devices, the material world would eventually come to a natural end. Since God is omnipotent, either he could allow this process to take place or he could take action (like the Flood) to accomplish that result. But it is not God's nature to let destruction take place (*Conf.* 181). For Philo the world is indestructible simply because God does not choose to destroy it.[22] This is certainly the import of Philo's approving citation of the *Timaeus:*

> ...the works of which I am the Maker and Father are indissoluble unless I will otherwise. Now all that is bound can be loosed but only the bad would will to loose what is well put together and in good condition (*Timaeus* 41a, as cited in *Aet.* 13).

---

[22]After saying in *Decal.* 58 (quoted above) that the genesis of the world is the beginning of its destruction, Philo adds: "even though by the providence of God it be made immortal...."

In *Her.* 246, Philo remarks that some people think the universe will be destroyed; others "declare that though by nature destructible (*phtharton*) it will never be destroyed, being held together by a bond of superior strength, namely the will of its Maker." The latter view is Philo's.

The opponents of the third article of the creed assert that the world is everlasting. The grounds of their assertion should not be confused with Philo's. They do not believe that God, impelled solely by his own goodness, chooses to allow the world to exist forever. Instead, they introduce a principle which is more active than God (cf. Philo's description of Stoic fire in *Aet.* 8-9), a principle which is able to shape the destiny of the world.[23] By this manoeuvre the majesty of God is undermined. And so, when Philo formulated the third article of the creed, he called to mind opposition from this quarter.

Those who refuse to believe in God as a creative or active force, those who would deny his power to destroy the world as well as his goodness in refraining from doing so, are not making a small doctrinal error. They are repudiating the essential nature of God and Moses' inspired account of creation. Philo was often

---

[23]Winston, in a private communication, notes that Philo appears to be referring here to late unidentified Stoics who "tried to escape from the theological dilemma by affirming that the Demiurge only creates the world and that not he, but fire destroys it." (J. Mansfeld, "Bad World and Demiurge," *Studies in Gnosticism and Hellenistic Religions* [Leiden, 1981], p.307). See also A. A. Long, "The Stoics on World Conflagration and Everlasting Recurrence," *Spindel Conference 1984: Recovering the Stoics*, ed. R. H. Epp, *The Southern Journal of Philosophy* (1985), vol. 23, supplement, pp. 13-39.

willing to bend Scripture to the needs of the moment. But confronted with the atheism of a determined opposition, Philo was not willing to make concessions. The third article of the creed explores and counters these unorthodox views.

(4) "*He has made it one world,*[24] *unique as Himself is unique*"

Philo's full statement of the fourth article of the creed is given in *Op.* 171:

> Fourthly, that the world (*kosmos*) too is one as well as its Maker, who made His work like Himself in its uniqueness, who used up for the creation of the whole all the material that exists.... For there are those who suppose that there are more worlds than one, while some think that they are infinite in number. Such men are ... lacking in knowledge....

This article has caused a certain amount of difficulty for the interpreters of Philo. For instance, it is the only article in the creed for which Wolfson was not able to construct a derivation from Scripture.[25] According to Wolfson, far from insisting on a unique world, Native Judaism was comfortable with the idea that, at the creation of our world, God created 196,000 other worlds.[26] What is more, while several ideas in this article of the creed draw

---

[24]This section depends on several passages in which the Loeb translators render *kosmos* as "world." In my discussion I have followed them in this usage. But perhaps that concept would be better rendered as "ordered universe."

[25]Wolfson, *Philo*, I, 180-81.

[26]*Idem.*

their inspiration from Plato,[27] Philo's reason for giving this issue such prominence is not derived from Plato.

Philo is explicit about the views of the opposition. Those who oppose this article believe in a plurality of worlds, and modern commentators agree that Philo must have had atomists in mind here.[28] If the identity of the opposition is clear, it is not so clear why Philo should take a stand on what appears to be a relatively unimportant philosophical point. The key to the problem lies in Philo's notion that if anything did exist outside our world--another world for instance--it would threaten the world we know with destruction (cf. *Timaeus* 33a). Since that was intolerable to Philo (cf. third article of the creed), he had to insist that beyond our world there is nothing and, as a corollary, that God made only one world.

Let us see in some detail how Philo argues for the latter position or, to be more precise, how that position fits into a critical cluster of ideas. In *Aet.* 20, we read:

> All things which are liable to perish are subject
> to two fundamental sources of destruction, the
> external and the internal.

Now the world cannot be destroyed by an internal force because this would imply that "the part would be greater and stronger

---

[27]For the idea of the uniqueness of the world and the use of all the material, see *Timaeus* 32c (quoted by Philo in *Aet.* 25-26). These ideas are also expressed elsewhere in Philo: *Prov.* frag. 1; *Det.* 154-55; *Post.* 5; *Plant.* 6-7.

[28]See Colson's note on *Op.* 170-71, *PLCL* 1, 476.

than the whole, which is against all reason" (*ibid.* 22).[29] Likewise, the world cannot be destroyed by an external force because there *is* nothing beyond the world we know. As Philo says elsewhere:

> ...this world (*kosmos*) of ours was formed out of all that there is of earth, and all that there is of water, and air and fire, not even the smallest particle being left outside (*Plant.* 6).

Since both internal and external means of destruction are precluded, the world itself must not be liable to perish (cf. *Aet.* 21).

As we can see, Philo's argument for the indestructibility of the world depends on the belief that there is nothing outside it. And if, indeed, there is nothing outside to destroy the world, then we must recognize the power of God to maintain it through his Logos (*Plant.* 7-8). In this group of interrelated ideas we find Philo's grounds for insisting on the uniqueness of the God's material creation.

(5) *"He ever exercises forethought for his creation"*

Philo presents the last article of the creed in these terms:

> Fifthly, that God also exercises forethought (*pronoei*) on the world's behalf. For that the Maker should care for the thing made is required by the laws and ordinances of Nature, and it is in accordance with these that parents take thought beforehand for children (*Op.* 171-72).

---

[29] In *Aet.* 22-24, Philo gives his argument that nothing internal will cause the destruction of the world; also see *Aet.* 74.

Having established God's role as creator in the preceding article, Philo now emphasizes that God's providential care for the world does not abate.[30] Philo makes the same point in *Prov.* 2.2-6. Here God is depicted as combining the characteristics of a sovereign with those of a father. God continues to exhibit providential concern for his children even when their behavior leaves something to be desired:

> Now parents do not lose thought for their wastrel children but ... bestow on them care and attention (*ibid*. 4).

The paternal aspect of God is a significant part of his being.

Modern commentators agree that the last article of the creed was written in opposition to the Epicureans and those under their influence.[31] In order to fill out our picture of the Epicurean opposition, we should turn to *LA* 3.28-31 where Philo discusses Gen. 3:8, the scene in which Adam and Eve hide from God:

> ...he that runs away from God declares Him to be the cause of nothing, and himself to be the cause of all things that come into being. The view, for instance, is widely current that all things in the world tear along automatically independently of anyone to guide them, and that the human mind by itself established arts,

---

[30]Winston, in a private communication, provides the following note on God's forethought: "Cf. *Agr.* 51; *Ebr.* 199; *Conf.* 98; *Abr.* 70; *Spec.* 2.260; 3.189; *Praem.* 32-34; *QG* 4.88; *QE* 2.64; Seneca, *Ep.* 58.28; Plutarch, *Mor.* 927 AC; Apuleius, *De Plat.* 205-206; Ps.-Plutarch, *De Fato* 573 AC. The staunchest proponent among the Middle Platonists of the doctrine of divine Providence is Atticus, fr.4. See Runia, *Philo...*, I, 206-207."

[31]Colson (in *PLCL* 1, 476) directs readers to Diogenes Laertius 10.77,113,139.

> professions, laws, customs, and rules of right treatment... (*LA* 3.29-30).

The miscreant depicted above has all the earmarks of one who rejects providence. The picture of the world moving along without a guide is familiar from Epicurean writings. Interestingly enough, in this passage Philo links disbelief in providence with total rejection of God. In fact Epicureans had no difficulty separating these ideas, and they were able to affirm the existence of the gods, while denying divine providence. For Philo, however, these two ideas were inextricable.

This concludes our review of the articles of the creed as presented in *Op.* 170-172. In addition to what has already been said, two general considerations suggest that this passage is crucial. First of all, the passage is placed at the culmination of *De Opificio*, perhaps Philo's most profound work. Equally significant is the frequency with which Philo returns to the five basic issues elsewhere in his corpus. In his discussion of the Tower of Babel, for instance, Philo characterizes the beliefs of those who raised their hands against heaven:

> For in fact that tower not only has human misdeeds for its base, but it seeks to rise to the region of celestial things, with the arguments of impiety and godlessness in its van. Such are its pronouncements, either that the Deity does not exist, or that it exists but does not exert providence, or that the world had no beginning in which it was created, or that though created its course is under the sway of varying and random causation... (*Conf.* 114).

Each of the categories of anomie mentioned here may be correlated with one of the articles of the creed. Likewise, in *Spec.* 1. 324-26, Philo mentions several classes of sinners who are unworthy of entering the holy congregation (cf. Deut. 23:1f.). In Philo's allegorical interpretation (*Spec.* 1.327-45), these sinners become those who overstep doctrinal bounds. Among the unworthy are those who do not accept incorporeal ideas (*ibid*. 327-29). But with this addition, all the other doctrinal sins described here can be found in the *De Opificio* creed. From such passages, it is clear that Philo's statements in *Op.* 171-72 constitute a well formulated basis of his religious experience.

No claim is made here that this list is comprehensive or that it would exhaust Philo's thoughts on the subject of Jewish orthodoxy. While other investigators might define Philo's orthodoxy by listing different or even more beliefs, our knowledge of his orthodoxy would not necessarily be extended thereby. For even when we limit ourselves to five articles, there already is a convergence of ideas. In fact, if Philo had been so inclined, he might have stated that the alpha and the omega of orthodoxy was a belief in monotheism. The rest for him was commentary.

III. ORTHOPRAXY

Philo does not address the issue to be discussed in this chapter in an explicit, systematic fashion. Instead of beginning with texts, then, let us imagine for a moment a fanciful situation. On a sea voyage, Philo suffers the fate of many of his contemporaries and finds himself shipwrecked and cast up on an alien shore. Sympathetic natives inform him that nearby there is a small community of people like himself. How could Philo identify this community as Jewish? We already have some idea of what beliefs Philo would expect to find among men reputed to be his co-religionists. They would, of course, have the Torah, but what specific observances would Philo expect them to have culled from the Torah's many commands and prohibitions?[1] What would they have to *do* before Philo could identify them as Jews? Unfortunately no passage springs to mind which would facilitate a discussion on orthopraxy in the way that the *De Opificio* creed facilitated our investigation of orthodoxy. To answer these questions, we shall have to identify practices in the Philonic corpus which are necessary and sufficient for the existence of Jewish life and the preservation of Jewish identity.

Philo was well aware of diversity within Judaism. In his native city of Alexandria, there were extreme Jewish allegorists and more simple-minded literalists.[2] In public, Philo accepts the diversity they represent; that is, he seems to have regarded his disagreements with them as an internal matter. Even when he

---

[1] Cf. *Mos.* 2.46. See Runia, *Philo*..., I, 12-5.

[2] See Mack, "Philo and Exegetical Traditions...," pp. 240-43, esp. n. 43, and Shroyer, "Alexandrian Jewish Literalists."

criticizes the extremists (cf. *Mig.* 89-93), he does not question their allegiance to the Jewish people. Nor does he repudiate his own ties to them. At some point, however, diversity within the group reaches a natural limit. When diversity threatens the group's sense of itself, Philo draws the line.

Spec. 1.54-57 gives a case in point. That passage paints a vivid picture of men "consorting with foreign women and through the attraction of their love-charms spurning their ancestral customs and seeking admission to the rites of a fabulous religion" (*ibid.* 56). First of all, Philo would regard each of these activities as a transgression; each goes beyond the limits of tolerance. It is no wonder, then, that Philo speaks approvingly of the death penalty meted out to these particular transgressors (*ibid.* 57).

One indication that Philo takes an injunction seriously is when failure to observe it entails a communal sanction. In *Spec.* 1.54-57, the sanction is death. As far as the community is concerned, this is equivalent to declaring that someone is an apostate or placing him beyond the pale.[3] All these sanctions re-assert the authority of the group and re-affirm its identity. The issue of orthopraxy in Philo thus involves several critical questions. What did one do, from Philo's vantage point, to stay in the community? What did one have to do (or fail to do) to be excluded from the community? Or, to return to the imaginary community mentioned above: what practices would Philo recognize

---

[3]Cf. *Spec.* 1.315-16: having fraternized with the multitude the transgressor is punished like a "public and general enemy." He is put to death.

as necessary and sufficient to identify an individual or group as Jewish?

It is not difficult to discern in *Spec.* 1.54-57 one aspect of Philo's concept of crime and appropriate punishment. Our task would be made much simpler if Philo told his readers in a systematic way which crimes were worthy of death and which deserved other forms of punishment. Unfortunately, the Philonic corpus does not yield its secrets so easily. We shall have to start, instead, by asserting what Philo must have held: to wit, that not every prohibition or command of the Torah is equally important.[4] That is, one's affiliation to the Jewish people is not put to the test by every biblical injunction. Philo is capable of bending, allegorizing, or rationalizing away those injunctions which do not conform to his conception of Judaism. On the other hand, he still considers the observance of certain prohibitions and commands to be an essential part of one's religious affiliation. If we can determine where Philo drew the line here, we shall have a key to his conception of Jewish identity.[5]

---

[4]Contrast the view expressed in *Pirke Avoth* II, 1: "Be heedful of a light precept as of a grave one, for thou knowest not the grant of reward for each precept" (trans. J.H. Hertz; New York, 1945).

[5]A most useful statement on drawing the line is made in G. Forkman, *The Limits of the Religious Community: Expulsion from the Religious Community within the Qumran Sect, within Rabbinic Judaism, and within Primitive Christianity* (Lund, 1972), pp. 10-13.

Circumcision

Philo's most remarkable reference to circumcision may be found at the beginning of *De Specialibus Legibus*. The general structure of that treatise is straightforward: Philo uses the Ten Commandments as ten headings under each of which he discusses a related group of Jewish practices and laws. Sometimes the items he raises for discussion seem to be quite appropriate to the heading or commandment. For instance, the first commandment provides Philo with a fitting occasion to denounce astral determinism, to affirm the act of creation, and so on. On other occasions, the "fit" seems more forced, as when he classifies the dietary laws under the tenth commandment. But even if he has to stretch a point, Philo presumably finds a berth under one commandment or another for every law of importance to him. It is noteworthy, then, that the one exception to Philo's classifications has to do with circumcision. In this one case, instead of subordinating the topic to one of the commandments, Philo inserts it very prominently at the beginning of the first book of *De Specialibus Legibus*, *before* his treatment of the first commandment. From the exceptional placement of his remarks, there is good reason to suppose that circumcision is a central issue for Philo.

In his discussion of circumcision, Philo first acknowledges an undercurrent of ridicule "among many people" (*Spec.* 1.1-2). His immediate response was to argue that the Jews were not the only people who practiced the rite.[6] As readers of Herodotus

---

[6] Also see *QG* 3.47-48.

(2.104) knew, circumcision was familiar to the Egyptians.[7] So Philo reminds his readers that the Egyptian race was regarded "as pre-eminent for its populousness, its antiquity and its attachment to philosophy" (*Spec.* 1.2). This historical observation clearly could be used to silence detractors (cf. *ibid.* 3).

Philo's remarks about circumcision were addressed to two distinct audiences. First there were non-Jewish detractors who maligned whatever they regarded as strange in Judaism. Philo took their attacks seriously, as we shall see in detail in the following chapter. Then there were critics of the rite who came from within Judaism itself. In *Mig.* 89-93, for example, Philo refers to certain Jews who emphasize the symbolic meaning of circumcision at the expense of its literal sense.[8] He does not wish to deny the symbolic level:

> It is true that receiving circumcision does indeed portray the excision of pleasure and all passions, and the putting away of the impious conceit, under which the mind supposed that it was capable of begetting by its own power... (*Mig.* 92).[9]

---

[7]Cf. Winston, *Selections*, pp. 385-86, nn. 634-35.

[8]Circumcision is not the only Jewish practice mentioned here. Significantly, Philo also refers to Sabbath and festival observance and an awareness of the sanctity of the Temple. Obviously, *Mig.* 89-93 gives us some idea of Philo's priorities. On the danger of a "pure spiritualization of the Torah," see G. Scholem, *On the Kabbalah and Its Symbolism* (trans. R. Manheim; New York, 1965), pp. 52-53.

[9]The same symbolic values are stressed in *Spec.* 1.8-10; *QG* 3.46-48,52,61; *QE* 2.2.

At the same time, he adds:

> ...but let us not on this account repeal the law laid down for circumcising (*ibid.*).

The Jews who emphasized the symbolic meaning of circumcision belonged to a new class. They seem to have regarded themselves as liberal and rational or, in a word, as "modern." We can infer this from the fact that Philo does not try to convince them by traditional arguments. For them it was not sufficient simply to assert, citing Gen. 17: 9-14, that Jews should circumcise their sons. Instead Philo points to the alleged practical advantages of the rite--health and fertility.[10]

Another informative passage, *QG* 3.52, is a commentary on LXX Gen. 17:14. That verse reads:

> And the uncircumcised male, who shall not be circumcised in the flesh of his foreskin on the eighth day, that soul (*hē psychē*) shall be utterly destroyed from its people (*tou genous*), for he has broken my covenant *(tēn diathēkēn)*.

Now even a cursory look at Gen. 17:14 indicates that, when a child has not been circumcised, communal sanctions must be invoked. But against whom should they be directed? Philo is

---

[10]Philo again cites health and fertility as reasons for circumcision in *QG* 3.48. Borrowing a phrase from William James, M. Douglas calls this kind of argumentation "medical materialism"; see her *Purity and Danger: An Analysis of Concepts of Pollution and Taboo* (London, 1966), pp. 29-32.

Goodenough's remarks on *Spec.* 1.1-2 also are of interest: "here appears for the first time so far as I know the myth that circumcision was originally given to the Jews, or practised by them, for hygienic reasons" (*Introduction,* p. 41).

aware of one school of thought which states that the uncircumcised child himself must suffer punishment. As the following rhetorical question records, Philo objects to this:

> But if the child is not circumcised on the eighth day after birth, what sin has he committed that he should be judged deserving of suffering death (*QG* 3.52)?

In Philo's view, the parents must be held responsible, and the passage just cited continues in that vein:

> Accordingly, some say that the law of interpretation has in view the parents, for it believes that they show contempt for the commandment of the law. Others, however, say that it has imposed a very excessive penalty on infants, it seems, and that those adults who disregard and violate the law are deserving of punishment without regret or remission (*ibid.*).

What is significant here is that Philo does not see circumcision simply as a ritual whereby a male child gains entry into the congregation of Israel. The focus, instead, is on the spirit of compliance or non-compliance in the parents. The difference is crucial and characteristic of Philo.

But what of the child who has been denied circumcision? His transgression, if it may be called that, is external and may be rectified. Essentially, he would not differ from the proselyte[11] whose uncircumcision is not a disgrace. Such a person

> ...is one who circumcises not his uncircumcision but his desires and sensual pleasures and the other passions of the soul. For in Egypt the

---

[11] For the use of "proselyte" here see Marcus' note *c* in *PLCL* supple. 2, p. 36 and the fragment, *ibid.*, p. 240.

> Hebrew nation was not circumcised but being mistreated with all (kinds of) mistreatment by the inhabitants..., it lived with them in self-restraint and endurance... (*QE* 2.2).

Neither proselytes nor uncircumcised children are threats to the social order. Like the ancient uncircumcised Jews who were slaves in Egypt, they evoke a sympathetic response from Philo. The same cannot be said, however, of parents who refuse to extend the rite to their children. They deserve a severe penalty presumably for showing contempt for the Torah and jeopardizing the survival of Judaism. Their refusal constitutes a clear case of overstepping the limits of tolerance.

Philo's discussions of circumcision indicate that the practice was of prime importance to his conception of Jewish orthopraxy. His writings on the subject have a sense of urgency, for he saw circumcision not only attacked from without, but also undermined from within.[12]

Sabbath

When Philo expresses his disapproval of those who take the literal prescriptions of the Torah in a purely symbolic sense,[13]

---

[12] See P. Borgen, "Debates on Circumcision in Paul and Philo" in *Philo, John and Paul; New Perspectives on Judaism and Early Christianity* (Atlanta, 1987), pp. 61-71, 233-54, and especially R. D. Hecht, "The Exegetical Contexts of Philo's Interpretation of Circumcision: in *Nourished with Peace: Studies in Hellenistic Judaism in Memory of Samuel Sandmel*, ed. F. E. Greenspahn *et al.* (Chico, 1984), pp. 51-79. I am indebted to D. Winston for calling my attention to these references.

[13] Cf. *Mig.* 89-93.

circumcision is not the only issue he mentions. The observance of the sabbath seems to be equally important:

> It is quite true that the Seventh Day is meant to teach the power of the Unoriginate and the non-action of created beings. But let us not for this reason abrogate the laws laid down for its observance, and light fires or till the ground or carry loads or institute proceedings in court or act as jurors or demand the restoration of deposits or recover loans, or do all else that we are permitted to do as well on days that are not festival seasons (*Mig.* 91).

This passage mentions two classes of prohibitions: those related to a Jew's domestic life and those related to his civic life. The domestic activities (lighting fires, tilling the ground, and carrying loads) may have been singled out because each of them has a public character. Lighting fires was a particularly serious offense, as a man who gathered firewood on the sabbath learned to his cost (cf. Num. 15:32-36). That deed, Philo explains,

> covered practically all the prohibitions enacted for the honouring of the seventh day. How is this? Because not merely the mechanical but also the other arts and occupations, particularly those which are undertaken for profit and to get a livelihood, are carried on directly or indirectly by the instrumentality of fire (*Mos.* 2.218-19).[14]

Philo's discussion of this particular incident is interesting because in it he also indicates what contemporary Jews were actually expected to do on the sabbath: to wit, "occupy themselves with the philosophy of their fathers, dedicating that time to the

---

[14] On the prohibition of sabbath fires, see *Spec.* 2.65.

acquiring of knowledge and the study of the truths of nature" (*ibid.* 216).[15]

The other activities mentioned in *Mig.* 91 also involve Jews in public acts. Philo suggests that his co-religionists refrain from all activities on the sabbath which have a bearing on their civic or business lives. In asking Jews to recognize the sabbath in this way, Philo is simply affirming a position which the civic authorities themselves either adopted or, in his view, should have adopted. The emperor Tiberius, for instance, is depicted as going out of his way to cater to Jewish sensibilities by granting special dispensations to Roman Jews:

> ...in the monthly doles in his own city when all the people... receive money or corn, he never put the Jews at a disadvantage in sharing the bounty, but even if the distributions happened to come during the sabbath when no one is permitted to receive or give anything or to transact any part of the business of ordinary life, particularly of a lucrative kind, he ordered the dispensers to reserve for the Jews till the morrow the charity which fell to all (*Legat.* 158).

---

[15] Philo's views of proper activity for Jews on the Sabbath are discussed more fully in my *SEPA*, pp. 32-33. R. Goldenberg, "The Jewish Sabbath in the Roman World up to the Time of Constantine the Great," *ANRW* 19.1, 429, notes that there was no universal agreement among Jews as to how the sabbath should be observed: "The *halakhah* varied ... from place to place and from group to group." Goldenberg also makes the important point (*ibid.*) that with the exception of Philo's "allegorizing opponents," all groups agreed that "Scripture must be the basis of any form of Judaism, and Scripture insists on the Sabbath as a central pillar of life under the covenant."

This is not to suggest that what Tiberius allegedly did in Rome was mirrored elsewhere in the Empire. Yet the Jews of Alexandria did enjoy certain sabbath privileges, as is clear from the case of a local governor who tried to rescind them:

> Not long ago I knew one of the ruling class who when he had Egypt in his charge and under his authority purposed to disturb our ancestral customs and especially to do away with the law of the Seventh Day which we regard with most reverence and awe. He tried to compel men to do service to him on it and perform other actions which contravene our established custom, thinking that if he could destroy the ancestral rule of the Sabbath it would lead the way to irregularity in all other matters, and a general backsliding (*Somn.* 2.123).

In response to the governor's challenge to the sabbath, the Jews "were intensely indignant and shewed themselves as mournful and disconsolate as they would were their native city being sacked and razed, and its citizens being sold into captivity..." (*ibid.* 124). This passage illustrates in a most dramatic way the strength of Philo's attachment to sabbath observance and his belief in the sabbath as a cornerstone of Jewish practice.

We may conclude from *Legat.* 158 and *Somn.* 2.123 that Philo expected the civic authorities to respect the Sabbath. It follows from this that Philo would have expected Jews to respect their own day of rest, for if on the Sabbath individual Jews conducted their businesses as usual, then the system whereby the Jewish community was granted certain privileges by the civic authorities would be undermined. That, in turn, would have serious repercussions because in Roman times a Jew lived and thought of himself in terms of the privileges granted to his people.[16]

Festivals, Sacrifice, and the Day of Atonement

In this chapter we have begun to trace the lowest common denominator in Philo's concept of religious observance. While the rituals connected with circumcision and sabbath obviously are required of anyone calling himself Jewish, the same cannot be said for all the festivals of the calendar. Philo tends, first of all, to pick and choose between various festivals. This tendency itself was not a traditional alternative. It reflects the fact that Philo had to accommodate himself to life in the Diaspora. The compromises he was prepared to make stand out most clearly when we compare his views of ordinary festive occasions with his attitudes toward the Day of Atonement.

In *Sacr.* 63, Philo acknowledges that the Jews are bidden to observe the Passover. But instead of indicating what is involved in keeping the festival, Philo simply elaborates on the allegorical meaning of the word "passover." "Passover," he tells us, means "passage from the life of the passions to the practice of

---

[16]Cf. J.N. Sevenster, *The Roots of Pagan Anti-Semitism in the Ancient World* (Supplements to *Novum Testamentum*, vol. 41; Leiden, 1975), pp. 145-59. In his article, "The Jewish Sabbath ...," pp. 415ff., Goldenberg discusses the documents (reproduced in Josephus' *Ant.* 14 and 16) concerning the Jews' right to observe the Sabbath. On the subject of Jewish privileges, we should note Philo's awareness in *Legat.* 156-57 and *Spec.* 1.76 of the right of Jews to collect money for Jerusalem. Also see V. Tcherikover, *Hellenistic Civilization and the Jews* (trans. S. Applebaum; Philadelphia, 1959), pp. 306-308.

virtue."[17] This definition does not meet the practical needs of a Jew who wants to place the festival in a context of religious practice. In fact it helps to remove it from such context.

Paschal sacrifices are mentioned in *Spec.* 2.145-46.[18] This passage raises more questions than it answers, for when we compare it with Exod. 12, glaring discrepancies appear. Philo introduces his discussion with these remarks on the roles of the people vis-à-vis the priests:

> In this festival many myriads of victims... are offered by the whole people, old and young alike, raised for that particular day to the dignity of the priesthood. For at other times, the priests according to the ordinance of the law carry out both the public sacrifices and those offered by private individuals. But on this occasion the whole nation performs the sacred rites and acts as priest with pure hands and complete immunity (*Spec.* 2.145).

Philo then goes on to describe the Exodus, after which he continues:

> So exceedingly joyful were they that in their vast enthusiasm and impatient eagerness, they naturally enough sacrificed without waiting for their priest. This practice which on that occasion was the result of a spontaneous and instinctive emotion, was sanctioned by the law once in every year to remind them of their duty of thanksgiving (*ibid.* 146).

---

[17] For the same phenomenon, see *Her.* 192.

[18] The large number of Jews who observed the Passover in Jerusalem during Second Temple times is attested in both Josephus (*BJ* 2.280 and 6.420ff.) and the Talmud (*Pes.* 64b). Cf. Safrai, *Aliyah*, pp. 42-43.

Thus, in Philo's view, the paschal sacrifice commemorates not an act of divine mercy which took place before the Exodus, but rather a spontaneous celebration which occurred after it.[19] The emphasis in *Spec.* 2.145-46 is on the participation of the populace and the non-participation of priests both in the beginning and subsequently. Nor is this the only passage in which the role of the priests in Passover celebrations is minimized. In *Mos.* 2.224, Philo discusses the Passover in these terms:

> ...the victims are not brought to the altar by the laity and sacrificed by the priests, but, as commanded by the law, the whole nation acts as priest, each individual bringing what he offers on his own behalf and dealing with it with his own hands.

The most striking aspect of *Mos.* 2.224 is Philo's reference to a law governing the participation of the individual, for sacrifices by individuals are not prescribed either in Deut. 16 or in related biblical passages.[20] There is, to be sure, no evidence to suggest that paschal sacrifices were made in Alexandria or that Philo would have sanctioned them. Yet Philo's emphasis on the people and their freedom from the ministrations of temple priests points in the direction of a measure of religious autonomy on the part of Alexandrian Jewry. The Jews of Alexandria apparently instituted a new religious festival to honor the Greek Bible (Cf. *Mos.* 2.41-42). Philo's view of the Passover seems to have been inspired by the same spirit.

---

[19]Cf. *PLCL* 7, 396, n.*a*.

[20]Cf. Exod. 12:1-28, 43-51; 13:3-10; Lev. 23:5-8; Num. 9:1-5; 28:16-25.

The idea advanced above, that Philo consciously adapted Jewish tradition to the needs of his Alexandrian co-religionists, is borne out in his discussion of the Second Passover. This issue is raised in Num. 9:6-13 where a dispensation is offered to those who missed the Passover either because they were ritually impure or because they were on a journey abroad (LXX Num. 9:10: *en hodo makran*). In both of the situations mentioned here, one is prevented from sacrificing at the prescribed time for a transitory condition. When the ritual impurity passed or the traveller returned home, one was again in a position to sacrifice. Since the stated punishment for failing to sacrifice was to be cut off from the people (Num. 9:13), Philo's interest in the topic is natural. As before, his treatment of the problem is adapted to the situation of his co-religionists. More specifically, in *Mos.* 2.232, Philo extends the notion of being away on a journey to include those who have settled more or less permanently in foreign lands:

> For settlers abroad and inhabitants of other regions (*hoi xeniteuontes ē heterōthi oikountes*) are not wrongdoers who deserve to be deprived of equal privileges, particularly if the nation has grown so populous that a single country cannot contain it and has sent out colonies in all directions.

Obviously these lines were written with the needs of Alexandrian Jews in mind.

Philo's treatment of sacrifice in general is consistent with his reflections on the Passover. In discussing sacrifice, Philo emphasizes the spiritual state of the worshipper even at the expense of the offering itself. This is the thrust of *Mos.* 2.107-108:

> ...if the worshipper is without kindly feeling or justice, the sacrifices are no sacrifices, the consecrated oblation is desecrated, the prayers are words of ill omen with utter destruction waiting upon them. For, when to outward appearance they are offered, it is not a remission but a reminder of past sins which they effect. But, if he is pure of heart and just, the sacrifice stands firm, though the flesh is consumed, or rather, even if no victim at all is brought to the altar.

One of Philo's most striking formulations of this idea may be found in *Plant.* 108:

> He [God] turns His face away from those who approach with guilty intent, even though they lead to His altar a hundred bullocks every day, and accepts the guiltless, although they sacrifice nothing at all.[21]

Philo's Judaism thus was a religion in which the state of one's soul had priority over mere formalities, and intent was more important than deed. Both the pagan and the Jewish world provided him with disturbing examples of the antithesis. Philo responded by formulating a more profound concept of sacrifice.[22]

Philo's approach to the Passover and to ordinary sacrifice is characterized by a flexible and liberal spirit. Neither quality is evident in his treatment of the Day of Atonement. First of all, Philo stresses the paramount importance of that day by calling it

---

[21] This idea also appears in *Spec.* 1.203, 271-72, and 290. The Essenes, as Philo notes in *Prob.* 75, serve God "not by offering sacrifices of animals, but by resolving to sanctify their minds."

[22] On the spiritualization of the sacrificial cult, see Winston's references in *Selections*, p. 355, nn. 289 and 297.

"the greatest of the feasts... a Sabbath of Sabbaths, or as the Greeks would say, a seven of sevens, a holier than the holy" (*Spec.* 2.194). The Day of Atonement was to have a central place in the lives of Alexandrian Jews, for Philo says that the fast was "carefully observed not only by the zealous for piety and holiness but also by those who never act religiously in the rest of their life" (*Spec.* 1.186). To this Philo adds that even non-Jews showed "awe and reverence for the fast" (*Mos.* 2.23).

The Day of Atonement, then, had a unique position in Philo's calendar. A Jew who did not observe that day would have been, in Philo's eyes, less responsive to his own religion than the reverent non-Jews mentioned in *Mos.* 2.23. From this we may conclude that observing the Day of Atonement was part of the lowest common denominator of Philonic orthopraxy.

Dietary Laws

In the eleventh chapter of Leviticus, the children of Israel are informed which animals they are allowed to eat and which they are forbidden. In abbreviated form, this is how Scripture deals with the matter:

> The Lord spoke to Moses and Aaron and said, Speak to the Israelites in these words: Of all animals on land these are the creatures you may eat: you may eat any animal which has a parted foot or a cloven hoof and also chews the cud; those which have only a cloven hoof or only chew the cud you may not eat. These are: the camel, because it chews the cud but has not a cloven hoof: you should regard it as unclean; ... the pig, because it has a parted foot and a cloven hoof but does not chew the cud; you shall regard it as unclean. You shall not

> eat their flesh or even touch their dead bodies; you shall regard them as unclean (Lev. 11 :1-4, and 7-8).[23]

No further explanations are given.

Where Philo departs from the biblical text is in providing rational explanations and allegorical interpretations for these *ex cathedra* commands.[24] His discussions are calculated to justify God's classifications of the various animals. Not only did God, like a good Linnean, place every creature in the appropriate category, He did so with the clear moral purpose of improving the character of man. As Philo explains,

> At the same time he also denied to the members of the sacred Commonwealth unrestricted liberty to use and partake of the other kinds of food. All the animals of land, sea or air whose flesh is the finest and fattest, thus titillating and exciting the malignant foe pleasure, he sternly forbade them to eat, knowing that they set a trap for the most slavish of the senses, the taste, and produce gluttony, an evil very dangerous both to soul and body. For gluttony begets indigestion which is the source and origin of all distempers and infirmities (*Spec.* 4.100).[25]

At one time, the words of Scripture on prohibited animals may have been adequate. From Philo's treatment it is clear that simple commands, with appeals to tradition, no longer provided

---

[23]Translation: New English Bible.

[24]Cf. the allegorical interpretation of dietary laws in the *Letter of Aristeas* 128-71.

[25]Philo continues along these lines until *Spec.* 4.118.

sufficient reason for religious observance. Again, as in the discussion on circumcision, Philo appears to be directing his remarks to the "modern" Alexandrian Jew who prides himself on having a rational grasp of religious practice. To be sure, Philo does not mention this group explicitly, but there can be no doubt that such Jews would find his remarks useful.

Philo's references to the camel and the pig illustrate these points. In *Agr.* 131, Philo recalls that the camel is unclean. The traditional reason for this, given in Lev. 11:4, is simply that it does not have a split hoof. As an explanation, Philo finds this less than satisfactory:

> ...if we fix our eyes on the literal way of regarding the matter, I do not know what principle there is in the reason given for the camel's uncleanness; but, if we look to the way suggested by latent meanings there is a most vital principle (*Agr.* 131).

This passage indicates that Philo's first impulse is to provide a rational principle for an animal's being declared unclean. If he is unable to provide such a principle, as in the case of the camel, then he turns to allegory to provide at least a homiletic explanation.

In some cases, Philo attempts to reconstruct Moses' principles of selection. In particular, Philo wants to explain to his audience why Moses designated the pig as unclean.[26] For him, it was not sufficient to cite Lev. 11:7 and point to the fact that the pig does not chew its cud. Instead, Philo observes that "among the different kinds of land animals there is none whose

---

[26] See Douglas, *Purity and Danger*, Ch. 3.

flesh is so delicious as the pig's..." (*Spec.* 4.101). Such a tempting animal can titillate one's desires and produce gluttony. Philo then argues that Moses was acting in the best interests of the Jews when he forbade them to eat the pig. Likewise the lawgiver prohibited the consumption of carnivorous animals, especially those which feed on human flesh. These animals "provide a very appetizing and delectable repast" (*ibid.* 103), but they are banned because of the ill effect they would have on the spirits of men. There is an important message here for Philo's "modern" co-religionists. They should realize that the list of unclean animals which appears in Scripture (Lev. 11:1-23 and Deut. 14:3-20) was not drawn up arbitrarily, but rather through a process of reasoning. In the same vein, Philo maintains that in drawing up his list of approved animals Moses "adhered to the principles of numerical science" (*Spec.* 4.105; cf. Deut. 14:4).

Philo's historical writings record two incidents in which the Jews' refusal to eat pork is taken as a touchstone. During the Alexandrian pogrom of the year 38 c.e., Jewish women were arrested and were ordered to eat pork, the archetype of unclean meat:

> ...the women who in fear of punishment tasted the meat were dismissed and did not have to bear any further dire maltreatment. But the more resolute were delivered to the tormentors to suffer desparate ill-usage...(*Flac.* 96).

Later when Philo was defending the interests of the Jewish community in an audience with Gaius, the emperor asked, "Why do you refuse to eat pork?" (*Legat.* 361). Gaius' question was greeted by an "outburst of laughter from some of our opponents" (*idem*). The Jewish delegation replied that "different people have different customs" (*ibid.* 362).[27] The non-Jews present seem to have found the situation very amusing; Philo himself felt quite the opposite (*ibid.* 363). Thus the prohibition against pork was well-known to those who would taunt the Jews. By Philo's time, refusal to eat it was already a test of Jewish courage and a mark of Jewish identity.

Intermarriage

Philo's discussion of the Sixth Commandment contains a review of forbidden unions (*Spec.* 3.12-31). For the most part, Philo's treatise follows the biblical prohibitions. *Spec.* 3.29 is significant, then, for Philo leaves the text of Lev. 18 to discuss the serious matter of intermarriage.

> ....do not enter into the partnership of marriage with a member of a foreign nation, lest some day conquered by the forces of opposing customs you surrender and stray unawares from the path that leads to piety and turn aside into a pathless wild (*Spec.* 3.29).

Philo grants that for one generation it might be possible to retain a Jewish way of life. The problems arise in the second:

> It may well be that they [the second generation], enticed by spurious customs which they prefer to the genuine, are likely to unlearn the honour due to the one God, and that is the first and the last stage of supreme misery (*ibid.*).

---

[27]Cf. *Letter of Aristeas* 180-81.

One scriptural authority for the prohibition of intermarriage is Deut. 7:3-6. In these verses, intermarriage is seen as tantamount to serving other gods. The punishment for such a transgression, as stated in Scripture, is divine wrath and destruction. Now if, as Philo suggests, intermarriage leads to a denial of monotheism, why does he fail to state what Scripture prescribes as the punishment for a union with one of another nation? Some insight into this question might be gained by examining Philo's treatment of several celebrated intermarriages: (1) Abraham and Hagar, (2) Jacob and his wives' maidservants, Bilhah and Zilpah, and (3) Moses and Zipporah.

(1) In the Book of Genesis, Sarah gave Hagar, her Egyptian maidservant, to Abraham as a wife (cf. *Congr.* 71 ff.). Despite this fact, Hagar has an air of unreality about her, for in concluding *De Congressu* Philo unceremoniously states that he has not been speaking about real women (i.e., Sarah and Hagar) at all, but rather about minds (*ibid*. 180). Elsewhere Philo does all he can to bring Hagar into the Jewish fold, stating that she may have been a slave outwardly, but "inwardly of free and noble race" (*Abr.* 251).[28] In the same spirit, we learn she may have been "an Egyptian by birth, but a Hebrew by her rule of life" (*ibid*.). This elevation of Hagar is not warranted by Scripture (cf. Gen. 16 and 21).

---

[28]Winston, in a private communication, refers readers to Genesis Rabbah 61.4 in which Hagar is seen as identical to Keturah. See J. Neusner, *Genesis Rabbah: The Judaic Commentary to the Book of Genesis...* vol. II (Atlanta, 1985), pp. 334f. It is interesting that Hagar's Egyptian origin is not discussed in the Midrash to Gen. 16:1 and 3.

(2) In *Virt.* 223, Philo seems to refer to Bilhah and Zilpah, "women born beyond the Euphrates, in the extreme parts of Babylonia." When they were deemed worthy, they "passed on from mere concubinage to the name and position of wedded wives, and were treated no longer as handmaids, but as almost equal in rank to their mistresses" (*ibid.*).[29] Again the elevation of these maidservants is not warranted by Scripture (cf. Gen. 30).

(3) Exod. 2:21 tells us that Moses married Zipporah, a woman from Midian. In Philo's study of the life of Moses, this marriage is mentioned in passing (*Mos.* 1.59). Perhaps because of the popular character of that treatise, however, Philo does not mention Zipporah by name; nor does he say anything about her, her status as a foreigner, or the intermarriage. In *LA* 2.67 the issue of her race does arise, but it simply becomes grist for Philo's allegorical mill. As in the case of Hagar, the woman herself is seen only as a virtue (*Cher.* 41).

In each of these cases, Philo either minimizes the foreign element in the marriage or ennobles the pagan partner. If we were to generalize from this evidence, we might conclude that, on a practical level, the alternative to intermarriage was conversion of the alien. This is also suggested by the surprisingly gentle tone taken in discussing the subject and the instances of biblical intermarriage, especially in view of the harsh condemnation of these practices in Deut. 7:3-6. It is, of course, impossible to

---

[29]Winston, in a private communication, refers to L. Ginzberg, *The Legends of the Jews* (7 vols.; Philadelphia, 1942) V, 295, n. 167. Winston also notes that, according to Demetrius the Chronographer, Zipporah was a descendant of Abraham.

know how often Alexandrian Jews were united by marriage with those born outside the faith. But Philo's laxness on the subject may be a sign that such unions were not unknown and that the better part of wisdom was to hope for the conversion of the non-Jewish partner.

Before concluding our study of Philo's concept of orthopraxy, we should take note of one more passage. In *Deus* 17-18, Philo writes:

> ...if there shall be any whose every deed is self-seeking, who have no regard for the honouring of their parents, for the ordering of their children aright, for the safety of their country, for the maintenance of the laws, for the security of good customs, for the better conduct of things private and public, for the sanctity of temples, for piety towards God, miserable shall be their fate. To sacrifice life itself for any single one of these that I have named is honour and glory.

Here Philo presents his readers with some basic elements of his faith. Several of them can easily be subsumed under principles of orthodoxy and orthopraxy discussed earlier. Even though Philo makes no attempt to present a systematic or comprehensive list,[30] this passage is significant. For in it Philo acknowledges that there are things in Judaism worth dying for. These elements are by definition at the core of the faith. To them we may add, as a minimal standard of Jewish practice, customs pertaining to

---

[30]In her edition of *De Congressu...* (vol. 16 of *Les oeuvres de Philon d'Alexandrie*, series ed. R. Arnaldez *et al.*; Paris, 1967), M. Alexandre suggests that Philo had a "repugnance for exhaustive accounts" (p.35).

circumcision, forbidden foods, the sabbath, the day of atonement, and intermarriage.

IV. PHILO'S APOLOGETIC

Theoretical Interlude

In his book on Jewish identity, Simon N. Herman makes the following point:

> When we discuss an individual's identity as it is shaped in the course of social interaction it is useful to distinguish...between objective public identity (a person's pattern of traits as they appear to others), subjective public identity (his perception of his appearance to others), and self-identity (the person's private version of his pattern of traits).[1]

So far in this essay we have concentrated almost exclusively on the third of Herman's classifications. That is, Philo's Judaism has been presented as if it were an abstract entity existing in a vacuum. Initially this approach was crucial because it allowed us to see the ideal. Unfortunately it does not take into account social realities. In the present chapter (and the following one as well), an attempt will be made to go beyond Philo's "private version" and to study the interaction between all three of Herman's classifications.

Another observation made by Herman would be appropriate for inclusion in this theoretical interlude: an individual's self-identity is influenced "by the way he believes others see him."[2] Since pagans made up the majority of the population of Alexandria, there is sufficient reason to explore the ways in which

---

[1] S.N. Herman, *Jewish Identity: A Social Psychological Perspective* (vol. 48 of the Sage Library of Social Research; Beverly Hills, 1977), p. 30.

[2] *Ibid.* p. 31.

pagans in Philo's environment influenced his sense of religious identity. To say that Philo was "influenced" by pagans does not mean that he was unfaithful as a Jew. On the contrary, as we have seen in previous chapters, the experience of living in the Diaspora seems to have heightened his awareness of belonging to the Jewish faith. What it *does* mean is that Philo had some kind of ongoing relationship with the pagan community.

Since other social scientists agree that the community would have an influence on a person in Philo's position, we should consider a formulation made by A.L. Epstein:

> Negative identity exists where the image of self rests chiefly on the internalized evaluations of others, and where accordingly much of one's behaviour is prompted by the desire to avoid their anticipated slights or censure. Positive identity, by contrast, is built on self-esteem, a sense of worthiness of one's own group's ways and values.... Yet even in the latter case what needs to be stressed is the way in which certain customs or practices which have come to be seen, both within and without the group, as diacritica of that group, so often turn out on closer inspection to reflect the group's relations with the wider society.[3]

"Negative identity," as it is defined here, is a useful concept for our inquiry into the way Philo thought of himself. For while I would not want to argue that Philo's image of himself rested *chiefly* on the "internalized evaluations of others," it will become obvious that his image of himself was shaped by such evaluations.

---

[3]Epstein, *Ethos and Identity*, p. 102. Also see P.L. Berger, and T. Luckmann, *The Social Construction of Reality* (London, 1967), p. 194.

At the source of this theorizing, there is an important assumption about the reciprocity of the relations between Jews and Gentiles. In my opinion we should not simply view the Jews of Philo's Alexandria as passive spectators on whom the social and political forces of the day worked their will. Rather, we should accept the fact that Alexandrian Jews were active participants-- actors on the historical stage who helped shape their environment. It is important to make this assumption explicit because it has not been easy for some modern commentators to think of the Jews as their Gentile neighbors saw them. I shall cite Jacob Katz's formulation of this issue since he writes with both authority and sensitivity:

> The relationship between Jews and Gentiles is at all times a reciprocal one. The behaviour of the Jews towards their neighbours is conditioned by the behaviour of the latter towards them, and vice versa. A real insight into this relationship can therefore be gained only by concentrating our attention simultaneously on both sides of the barrier. Every attitude of the Jew towards the non-Jew has its counterpart in a similar attitude of the Gentile towards the Jew.[4]

In this chapter, then, an attempt will be made to take reciprocity

---

[4]J. Katz, *Exclusiveness and Tolerance: Studies in Jewish-Gentile Relations in Medieval and Modern Times* (Oxford, 1961), p. 3. Also see the same author's *Tradition and Crisis: Jewish Society at the End of the Middle Ages* (New York, 1961), p. 11. Although these books deal mainly with medieval Jewry, I found them important for the light they shed on our subject.

seriously by viewing several topics (some of them already familiar) from the pagan side of the barrier.[5]

From the fourth century b.c.e. on, Greek ethnographers, philosophers, and historians commented on Jews and Judaism. We need only glance at the admirable collection of Menachem Stern to realize the extent of this Greek and Latin tradition.[6] Theophrastus (372-288/7 b.c.e.), perhaps the first pagan author to offer a general assessment of Judaism, declared that the Jews were a race of philosophers.[7] This early opinion was followed by many less complimentary ones, some of which challenged the very heart of Judaism.[8] Philo, always a keen observer of the fortunes of his people, was aware of these opinions and made an effort to respond

---

[5] Ralph Marcus was aware of the dynamic interplay of forces which produce anti-Semitism. In my view, he made every effort to view his subject from both sides of the barrier. See his essay "Antisemitism in the Hellenistic-Roman World" in *Essays in Antisemitism*, ed. K.S. Pinson (New York, 1946), pp. 61-78 (esp. p. 75).

[6] M. Stern, *Greek and Latin Authors on Jews and Judaism* (3 vols.; Jerusalem, 1976-84). Subsequent references to *GLA* will be of two kinds. (1) When I want to direct the reader's attention to a classical text in its entirety *and* the excellent notes which Stern supplies, I shall simply give the number assigned to that text (*e.g. GLA*, No. 1). (2) When I want to cite editorial remarks by Stern without reference to a particular text, I shall give the volume number and page (*e.g., GLA*, I, 5). It should be stated here that Stern's work has proved an invaluable aid to the study of Philo's Jewish identity.

[7] *GLA*, No. 4. See A. Momigliano, *Alien Wisdom: The Limits of Hellenization* (Cambridge, 1975), p. 92.

[8] Cf. Momigliano, "Greek Culture and the Jews" in *The Legacy of Greece: A New Appraisal*, ed. M.I. Finley (Oxford, 1981), p. 340.

to them. In so doing Philo altered the way he presented and perhaps the way he thought of his religion. For the Judaism of Philo's time was not shaped purely by an internal dialectic; it was also molded by pagan views of Jews and their customs.

In their attacks on Jews and Judaism, anti-Semitic[9] authors in antiquity often ridiculed practices which appeared offensive, peculiar, or simply incomprehensible. The dietary laws, the sabbath, and circumcision thus became grist for the anti-Semite's mill. These are issues which virtually every Jew considered essential to his faith. It is no coincidence that the anti-Semite should seize upon these very issues, for if he did not choose a sensitive point which lay at the heart of the matter, where was the sting of his attack?

Not every anti-Semitic allegation, however, corresponds in a straightforward way to specific Jewish practices. Some appear to be extrapolations from Jewish behavior as seen through the eyes of an unsympathetic social critic. We cannot afford to dismiss these allegations as groundless or irrelevant. For if we assume

---

[9] Good reasons have been offered for abandoning the use of the term "anti-Semitic." In retaining the term, I have accepted the position of Sevenster in his introduction to *Roots of Pagan Anti-Semitism*. Also see J.L. Daniel, "Anti-Semitism in the Hellenistic-Roman Period," *JBL* 98 (1979), 45-65 and S.J.D. Cohen, "'Anti-Semitism' in Antiquity : The Problem of Definition" in *History and Hate: The Dimensions of Anti-Semitism*, ed. D. Berger (Philadelphia, 1986), pp. 43-48. For a review of the literature on ancient Anti-Semitism, see L.H. Feldman, "Anti-Semitism in the Ancient World" in Berger, *History and Hate*, pp. 37-38, n. 1. Feldman is certainly correct when he argues that anti-Semitism was a "part of a varied and complex reality" which requires advanced analysis (*ibid*. p. 15).

that the relationship between Jews and non-Jews living in the same wider community is a reciprocal one, then it is important to investigate both sides of any issue. Even distorted views of Judaism might touch upon issues which would be close to the Jew's awareness of himself.

Before we proceed, it would be appropriate to say a few words about chronology. The analysis offered in this chapter does not depend on chronological sequences. Nor does it presume a linguistic compatibility between Philo and the author of a particular attack. Some of the charges leveled against Judaism have a long history which can be fully documented; others may find a voice in only one ancient source. Both sorts of charges are potentially relevant to Philo. Coming out of a world of rumor, slander, and suspicion, defamatory opinions tend to have long half-lives which transcend temporal, geographical, and linguistic barriers.[10] In studying them, we need only find some correlation between pagan views and Philonic apologetics. Such a correlation establishes a prima facie case for considering the issue further.

Indolence and the Sabbath

In this section, we shall explore the relationship between pagan conceptions of the sabbath and certain apologetic remarks by Philo. The sabbath, first of all, was the most conspicuous

---

[10]B. Wardy, "Jewish Religion in Pagan Literature during the Late Republic and Early Empire," *ANRW* 19.1, 613-15.

Jewish observance in the ancient world.[11] A fragment from the work of Agatharchides of Cnidus, an historian of the second century b.c.e., attests to this observance:

> The people known as Jews, who inhabit the most strongly fortified of cities, called by the natives Jerusalem, have a custom of abstaining from work every seventh day; on those occasions they neither bear arms nor take any agricultural operations in hand, nor engage in any other form of public service, but pray with outstretched hands in the temples until the evening (quoted in Josephus, *Apion.* 1.209).[12]

According to Agatharchides, the Jews, faithful to their sabbath laws, allowed Ptolemy Lagos to enter Jerusalem unopposed.[13] It is not difficult to see why laws which encouraged such remarkable behavior would stand out in a pagan's mind.

As the work of Stern indicates, various aspects of the sabbath caught the attention of non-Jewish authors.[14] We shall concentrate on indolence because both Philo and several pagan

---

[11] Goldenberg, "The Jewish Sabbath ...," p. 429. Also see Sevenster, *Roots of Pagan Anti-Semitism*, pp. 124ff.

[12] *GLA*, No. 30a.

[13] *GLA*, No. 30b.

[14] For some of the more telling references to the sabbath in the period prior to the second century c.e., see Stern, *GLA*: Meleager (No.43), Horace (No. 129), Pompeius Trogus (No. 137, sabbath as fast-day in 2.14), Ovid (No. 143), Apion (No. 165), Seneca the Philosopher (No. 188, sabbath lamps), Persius (No. 190, sabbath lamps), Martial (No. 239, sabbath as fast-day), and Plutarch (No. 258, sabbath wine in 6.2). Also see Goldenberg, "The Jewish Sabbath...," pp. 430-42.

writers comment on it. What the pagans appear to have been saying about the Jews may be inferred from the following three passages:

> Along with other superstitions of the civil theology Seneca also censures the sacred institutions of the Jews, especially the sabbath. He declares that their practice is inexpedient, because by introducing one day of rest in every seven they lose in idleness almost a seventh of their life, and by failing to act in times of urgency they often suffer loss... (view attributed to Seneca by Augustine, *De Civitate Dei*, 6.11).[15]

> They say that they first chose to rest on the seventh day because that day ended their toils; but after a time they were led by the charms of indolence to give over the seventh year as well to inactivity (Tacitus, *Historiae* 5, 4, 3).[16]

> Some who have had a father who reveres the Sabbath, worship nothing but the clouds, and the divinity of the heavens, and see no difference between eating swine's flesh, from which their father abstained, and that of man; and in time they take to circumcision.... For all which the father was to blame, who gave up every seventh day to idleness, keeping it apart from all the concerns of life (Juvenal, *Saturae* 14, 96-106).[17]

Apparently in response to charges such as these, Philo adopts an apologetic stance:

---

[15]*GLA*, No. 186.

[16]*GLA*, No. 281, p. 25.

[17]*GLA*, No. 301.

> On this day we are commanded to abstain from all work, not because the law inculcates slackness; on the contrary it always inures men to endure hardship and incites them to labour, and spurns those who would idle their time away.... Its object is rather to give men relaxation from continuous and unending toil and by refreshing their bodies with a regularly calculated system of remissions, to send them out renewed to their old activities. For a breathing-space enables not merely ordinary people but athletes also to collect their strength and with a stronger force behind them to undertake promptly and patiently each of the tasks set before them (*Spec.* 2.60).

Or, more succinctly, having discussed what is done on the sabbath in *Hypoth.* 7.10-13, Philo asks, "Do you think that this marks them as idlers...?" (*ibid.* 14). Just as Philo appeals to hygiene in justifying circumcision, so here he appeals to the physical benefits of observing the sabbath. In a curious anticipation of a modern work ethic, Philo insists that someone who rests on the sabbath can return rejuvenated and perform his work even more effectively than before. True, the body rests. But Philo is careful to point out that on the sabbath the soul does not rest (cf. *Spec.* 2.64; *Mos.* 2.215; *Op.* 128; *Cont.* 30-36). Indeed in *Dec.* 98, Philo recommends that Jews should use the sabbath to "consider whether any offence against purity had been committed in the preceding days, and exact from themselves... a strict account of what they had said or done...."

This is Philo's reply to the charge which found expression in pagan circles that the Jews institutionalized idleness on the sabbath. Although Philo never formulates this particular pagan charge in an explicit manner, he goes out of his way to emphasize that laziness has no part of Jewish observance. It can hardly be a coincidence that pagan writers make this accusation and that Philo denies it. But if Philo was consciously refuting a charge made against his people, why did he not attribute it to a contemporary pagan author? Two answers suggest themselves. First, the claim of Jewish sloth may have been a commonplace. Philo may have wished to play the accusation down so as not to lend it a dignity it did not deserve. The second alternative certainly would have been consistent with Philo's preferred mode of dealing with the external world by innuendo.[18] In the works which have come down to us, Philo (unlike Josephus in *Contra Apionem*) does not attempt to write an explicit, point-by-point refutation of charges leveled against the Jews. Nevertheless, confronted by either pagan misunderstanding or hositility, Philo addresses the issues with vigor.

Illicit Pleasures and Asceticism

One of the chief detractors of Judaism in antiquity was the Egyptian Apion. According to Josepus, Apion denounces the Jews "for sacrificing domestic animals and for not eating pork, and he derides the practice of circumcision" (*Apion*. 2.137).[19] Apion was not the only ancient who, if asked to characterize the Jews in a few words, would have mentioned circumcision. There is an irony in this for, as Josephus was quick to observe (*idem*), circumcision was practiced among the Egyptians as well as the Jews.

---

[18]Cf. Goodenough, *Politics*, Ch. 3.

[19]*GLA*, No. 176.

Nevertheless "for Greek and Latin writers the Jews were the circumcised *par excellence*."[20]

Among the pagan references to circumcision the most intriguing is that of Tacitus. In his *Historiae* 5.5, Tacitus appears to divide Jewish rites into two classes. Stern has described the first class as "rooted in the remote past of the Jews and given an aetiological explanation by Tacitus."[21] The second class includes customs which, according to Tacitus, are "base and abominable, and owe their persistence to their depravity" (*Historiae* 5.5.1). The following reflections on circumcision fall into the latter category:

> They sit apart at meals and they sleep apart, and although as a race, they are prone to lust, they abstain from intercourse with foreign women; yet among themselves nothing is unlawful. They adopted circumcision to distinguish themselves from other peoples by this difference. Those who are converted to their ways follow the same practice...(*ibid.* 5.5.2).

In this passage, Tacitus appears to conjoin the fact that the Jews practiced circumcision with a suggestion that they were lascivious

---

[20]*GLA*, I, 444. In Stern's collection, see the comments on circumcision made by the following authors: Herodotus (No. 1), Diodorus (Nos. 55, 57), Strabo (Nos. 115, 118), Persius (No. 190), Petronius (Nos. 194, 195) and Martial (Nos. 240, 245). Also see Winston, *Selections*, p. 385, nn. 634-35.

[21]*GLA*, II, 39.

by nature.[22] That pagans made this connection seems likely, especially when we consider Philo's repeated attempts to dissociate circumcision from illicit pleasure. For instance, in *De Specialibus Legibus* Philo argues that circumcision symbolizes

> ...the excision of pleasures which bewitch the mind. For since among the love-lures of pleasure the palm is held by the mating of man and woman, the legislators thought good to dock the organ which ministers to such intercourse, thus making circumcision the figure of the excision of excessive and superfluous pleasure, not only of one pleasure but of all the other pleasures signified by one, and that the most imperious (*Spec.* 1.9).[23]

Referring to Gen. 17:10, Philo asks why God commands that only male children should be circumcised (*QG* 3.47).[24] The first reason offered is that "the male has more pleasure in, and desire for, mating than does the female.... Therefore He rightly leaves out the female, and suppresses the undue impulses of the male by the sign of circumcision" (*ibid.*). The passage just cited reveals a certain ascetic streak in Philo's reflections on circumcision. Later

---

[22]Cf. Martial in *GLA*, No. 240, and comments by Daniel, "Anti-Semitism in the Hellenistic-Roman Period," p. 51. For a contrasting view to the one presented by me, see Sevenster, *Roots of Pagan Anti-Semitism*, p. 142.

[23]The theme of circumcision as the excision of pleasure is repeated in *Mig.92 and QE* 2.2. Also see *QG* 3.46 and 52. Winston, *Selections*, p. 386, n. 638, cites a similar sentiment by Maimonides.

[24]Some pagans thought that the Jews performed female excisions (cf. Strabo, *GLA*, Nos. 115 and 118). Philo may have been aware of this.

in *Quaestiones in Genesin* this undercurrent becomes even stronger. In reference to Gen. 17:24-25, Philo asks why Ishmael should be circumcised at the age of thirteen. The answer is that he is close to a marriageable age and anyone at that stage must

> ...circumcise his sense-pleasures and amorous desires, rebuking those who are lascivious and lustful, in order that they may restrain their excessive embraces, which usually come about not for the sake of begetting children but for the sake of unrestrained pleasure (*QG* 3.61).

Stern has noted that barbarians, especially those from the East, were commonly depicted as having strong sexual passions.[25] Philo does all he can to dissociate the Jews from any such depiction.[26] He attempts to do this not only by insisting that circumcision leads to self-restraint, but also more generally by adopting an ascetic view of sexual matters.

A logical place to start a discussion of asceticism in Philo is with his treatment of the commandment which proscribes adultery. Readers of the LXX must have been aware of some ambiguity about the place of this commandment. In the MT, the proscription of adultery is the seventh commandment (cf. Exod. 20:14 and Deut. 5:18). LXX Deut. 5 follows the MT in placing it seventh; LXX Exod. 20, however, departs from the MT by

---

[25]*GLA*, II, 40; Stern provides references from Tacitus and Justin.

[26]Philo tries to turn the tables by insisting that the Egyptians really were the licentious ones (cf. *Abr.* 107). For a similar theme in Josephus, see H.W. Attridge, *The Interpretation of Biblical History in the Antiquitates Judaicae of Flavius Josephus* (Harvard Dissertations in Religion 7; Missoula, 1976), pp. 126-37 and 173-75.

assigning adultery sixth place and murder seventh. Philo follows the latter version, which allows him to make the following point:

> In committing to writing the second set [of commandments] which contains the actions prohibited by our duty to fellow-men, He begins with adultery, holding this to be the greatest of crimes. For... it has its source in the love of pleasure (*philēdonian*) which enervates the bodies of those who entertain it, relaxes the sinews of the soul and wastes away the means of subsistence... (*Decal.* 121-22).

And again:

> The first commandment in the second table is "Thou shalt not commit adultery." It comes first, I think, because pleasure is a mighty force felt throughout the whole inhabited world (*Spec.* 3.8).

By advancing adultery to sixth place, Philo gives a certain prominence to that issue--even at the expense of diverting the reader's attention from the prohibition against murder. Philo may have done this because, of the two transgressions, adultery was a more pressing problem for the Alexandrian Jewish community. The gravity of adultery is emphasized by Philo's calling it "the greatest of crimes" (*Decal.* 121) and by his making no effort to mitigate the biblical punishment of death for transgressors (*Spec.* 3.11; cf. Lev. 20:10 and Deut. 22:22 where the death penalty is prescribed).[27] Philo tolerates no compromise here because the threat of adultery strikes at the very heart of community

---

[27]Cf. S. Belkin, *Philo and the Oral Law: The Philonic Interpretation of Biblical Law in Relation to the Palestinian Halakah* (Cambridge, 1940), Ch. X.

solidarity. As Philo's remarks on bastardy indicate (*Spec.* 3.11), adultery endangers the entire social fabric.

Since Philo thought that marriage was critical to the survival of the Jewish community and adultery undermined marriage, it was natural for him to condemn adultery in the strongest terms. But Philo does not stop there. He also stresses the idea of chastity *within* marriage, condemning men who "in their craze for sexual intercourse behave unchastely, not with the wives of others, but with their own" (*Spec.* 3.9). In advocating chaste marriages, Philo is not referring to restrictions on marital relations set forth in Lev. 15.[28] His idea may be explained by more explicit remarks made elsewhere:

> And because, with a view to the persistence of the race, you were endowed with generative organs, do not run after rapes and adulteries and other unhallowed forms of intercourse, but only those which are the lawful means of propagating the human race (*Det.* 102).

In *QG* 4.86 Philo adds that "an unpolluted marriage" is one which does not have "sensual pleasure as its end but the procreation of legitimate children." The marriage of Abraham and Sarah exemplifies this spirit, as Sarah is quick to explain in *Abr.* 248:

> Long have we lived together in mutual goodwill. But the purpose for which we ourselves came together and for which nature formed the union of man and wife, the birth of children, has not been fulfilled....

---

[28]Philo's extended discussion of adultery (*Spec.* 3.7-82) contains only one allusion (*ibid.* 63) to any provison of Lev. 15. Cf. Belkin, *Philo and the Oral Law*, pp. 219-23.

Philo obviously is not comfortable with the sexuality of his biblical heroes so he reiterates his ascetic ideal whenever he can. Concerning Abraham and Sarah, Philo adds in *Cong.* 12:

> In the present discussion, we must eliminate all bodily unions or intercourse which has pleasure as its object. What is meant is a mating of mind with virtue.

Likewise, Philo says of Moses that he bestowed

> ... on his belly ... no more than the necessary tributes which nature has appointed, and as for the pleasures that have their seat below, save for the lawful begetting of children, they passed altogether even out of his memory (*Mos.* 1.28).

Later Philo pictures Moses on the eve of his ascent to Mt. Sinai as completely devoid of passion:

> But first he had to be clean, as in soul so also in body, to have no dealings with any passion, purifying himself from all the calls of mortal nature, food and drink and intercourse with women. This last he had disdained for many a day, almost from the time when, possessed by the spirit, he entered on his work as prophet, since he held it fitting to hold himself always in readiness to receive the oracular messages (*Mos.* 2.68-69).

Philo may have been influenced to depict Moses in this way by the description of the preparations of the children of Israel before the theophany (Exod. 19:10-15). Yet a comparison of *Mos.* 2.68-69 with the biblical account available to Philo would reveal very few points in common, and one cannot help thinking that Philo wanted to make a special point of Moses' irreproachable sexual purity. Indeed at one point Philo even claims that the

Lawgiver did not represent the patriarchs and Moses as "knowing women" (*Cher.* 40).[29]

The logic of Philo's position leads him not only to protect the patriarchs from allegations of impurity,[30] but also to formulate various rules of conduct which go further in asceticism than Scripture itself.[31] For instance in *Spec.* 3.34-36, Philo denounces the licentious pleasure of mating with a barren woman. A man who does this deliberately is regarded as ploughing a "hard and stony land"; in Philo's estimation he is an enemy of nature. Granted that Philo does not sanction the dismissal of a wife who, after many years of companionship, proves incapable of bearing children (*ibid.* 35). But this is the only lenient touch in an

---

[29]Cf. *Cher.* 43-52 and Goodenough, *Light*, p. 201. On the sexual process in postbiblical Judaism see the remarks of R. Gordis, *The Book of Job: Commentary, New Translation, and Special Studies* (New York, 1978), pp. 522-23.

[30]Philo's concern to depict Moses as pure is a response to the pagan effort to depict him as diseased. Cf. *GLA*, Nos. 248 and 331. Also see Manetho's comment that at the Exodus the Jews were leprous (*GLA*, No. 21 = Josephus, *Apion.* 1.229).

[31]See I. Heinemann, *Philons griechische und jüdische Bildung* (Breslau, 1932), pp. 262-67, and Colson's note on *Spec.* 3.34-36 in *PLCL* 7, 633-34.

ascetic passage which has no biblical authority.[32]

Philo's treatment of prostitutes likewise goes further than Scripture. Without specifying any punishment, LXX Deut. 23:18 bans prostitutes from among the children of Israel (*ouk estai pornē apo thygaterōn Israēl*...). Philo, however, makes prostitution a capital offense: "...with us a courtesan (*hetaira*) is not even permitted to live, and death is the penalty appointed for women who ply this trade" (*Jos.* 43). In *Spec.* 3.51, Philo advocates stoning as the appropriate punishment for a woman who sells herself "like some ware to be purchased in the market." The severity of the punishment is apparently related to the social dislocation which Philo perceived to follow in the wake of prostitution.[33]

---

[32] See D. Sly, "The Perception of Women in the Writing of Philo of Alexandria" (unpublished Ph.D. dissertation, McMaster University, 1987), pp. 90-108 and 234-40. In the latter section Sly takes up the issue of Phineas and the Levites, whose depiction by Philo "goes beyond the demands of Scripture" (p. 236). Also see Goodenough, *Jurisprudence of Jewish Courts in Egypt* (New Haven, 1938), p. 89 (as noted by Sly), and Winston, *Selections*, pp. 368-69, n. 425. Winston's references here to both classical and rabbinic sources are particularly useful.

[33] The Hebrew word used in Deut. 23:18, *qedeshah*, carries the connotation of a sacred prostitute. (This understanding of the term is consistent with Deut. 23:19.) When Philo interprets LXX Deut. 23:18, he does not see any sacred function in the prostitute's activities. He takes *pornē* to mean harlot, prostitute, or strumpet (cf. Liddell and Scott). Thus Philo appears to be more strict with ordinary prostitution than the MT is with its sacred form. (DNM, 1982.) Also see Belkin, *Philo and the Oral Law*, pp. 258f., and Sly, "Perception of Women," pp. 247-49.

The social dimension of Philo's sexual ethic is also clear in his denunciation of incest and homosexuality. Incest, committed unknowingly by Oedipus, "produced such a harvest of ills that nothing was wanting that could lead to the utmost misery" (*Spec.* 3.15). Philo enumerates the ills: civil and foreign wars with great cities sacked, armed forces destroyed, brave leaders dead, and families torn apart by internecine feuding (*ibid.* 16).[34] Similarly, homosexuality renders cities "desolate and uninhabited by destroying the means of procreation" (*ibid.* 39).[35]

Philo's discussions of sexual misbehavior emphasize the social consequences of these acts. "The incitements to sexual indulgence... have ruined entire cities and countries and vast regions of the earth, as wellnigh all the poets and historians of the world testify" (*Det.* 99; cf. *Abr.* 133-41). As a member of a vulnerable minority Philo was eager to avert the devastation which illicit sexual activity might bring to the Jewish community. He was also concerned in a more apologetic way to combat the

---

[34]Cf. Colson's note in *PLCL* 7, 483.

[35]Cf. *Abr.* 135-36 and *Cont.* 59-62; also see Colson's note in *PLCL* 7, 498-99.

pagan charge that the Jews were a lascivious people.[36]

Virtually every passage quoted earlier in this section points to Philo's distrust of pleasure.[37] An examination of Philo on the subject of pleasure reveals that in fact he held two incompatible views. First it would appear that Philo was simply opposed to immoderate pleasure. This inference may be drawn from *LA* 3.111:

> ...when we have glutted ourselves with immoderate pleasure (*hēdonēs ametrou*), we cannot see nor hear nor smell nor taste nor feel with clearness, but our contact with objects of sense is dim and feeble.[38]

Here pleasure itself is not intrinsically evil. Since small pleasures are a necessity (cf. *LA* 2.17), it is sufficient if one simply tames one's desires for them. As Philo notes, the impulse to indulge in pleasures may, with the aid of reason, lead to a "noble victory of endurance and self-mastery, in a vigorous and pertinacious encounter with everything that excites the unruly desires" (*LA* 3.156).

---

[36]In *Spec.* 3.169-77, Philo discusses the desirability of female seclusion and modesty. The only exception to a Jewess' seclusion is when she goes to worship (*ibid.* 171). Heinemann has argued (*Bildung*, p. 234) that Philo's notions on this subject do not reflect Jewish ideas. He finds instead Greek influence (cf. *PLCL* 7, 640, n. 171). But if my analysis is correct, the decisive factor is Philo's apologetic mission. Philo could not have found a better way to counter the charges of lasciviousness than to champion the seclusion of Jewish women.

[37]See, for instance, *Spec.* 1.9; *QG* 3.4, 61; *Decal.* 121-22; *Spec.* 3.8-9; *Cong.* 12; *Mos.* 1.28.

[38]The same sentiment is expressed in *LA* 3.183-84.

Elsewhere, however, pleasure takes on a more sinister aspect. In Philo's interpretation of the Garden of Eden, the serpent becomes a symbol of pleasure. Pleasure no longer is a neutral force to be mastered. Rather it is an alien element in Philo's moral universe, "a courtesan and a wanton" (*hetairis kai machlas*, *Op*. 166).[39] As Philo writes in *LA* 3.68,

> ...the serpent, pleasure, is bad of itself; and therefore it is not found at all in a good man, the bad man getting all the harm of it by himself.[40]

Reason and pleasure are fundamentally incompatible: "when reason prevails pleasure is gone, and when pleasure conquers, reason is an exile" (*LA* 3.116).

In this spirit we come to *Sacr*. 20-32, Philo's allegory of two wives "who hate and loathe each other." One wife is Virtue, the other Pleasure. "Know then," says Virtue, "that if you become a pleasure-lover (*philēdonos*) you will be all these things..." (*ibid*. 32). Here follows perhaps the most extensive catalogue of

---

[39]Cf. *LA* 3.76.

[40]Here pleasure is contrasted with sense-perception which "comes under the head neither of bad nor of good things" (*LA* 3.67). Also see *ibid*. 107. To this Winston, in a private communication, adds: "Pleasure in these contexts connotes the irrational emotion rather than the neutral agreeable physical feelings as such, which are permitted even to the wise man." See Winston, "Philo's Ethical Theory" in *ANRW* 21.1, 408.

pleasure-related vices which has come down to us from antiquity. Man's duty is not to tame pleasure, but to avoid it entirely.[41]

Philo's reflections on asceticism and pleasure are so extreme and disjointed--in a sense they are so foreign to the spirit of the Bible--that one is tempted to inquire into non-Jewish influences. Have the ascetic views of Plato influenced Philo? First of all, the spirit of Plato's asceticism is very much in evidence in Philo's work. In *Somn.* 2.48-77, Philo denounces the vainglory of Joseph, "the enemy of simplicity and the friend of vanity" (*ibid.* 63). Plato is not specifically mentioned, but Philo's distinction between "the true and simple life" and "the life of falsity and vanity" (*ibid.* 64) is one which Plato would recognize. In other passages, there are distinct echoes of Platonic ideas. For instance in *Det.* 34 "lovers of virtue" are caricatured by their vicious opponents as "obscure people, looked down upon, of mean estate, destitute of the necessaries of life... filthy, sallow, reduced to skeletons... the prey of disease, in training for dying" (*meletōntes apothnēskein*). The last phrase is a clear reference to Plato's *Phaedo*.[42] Again in *Gig.* 14 Philo uses a Platonic phrase to portray the true philosopher as one who studies "to die to the life in the body."[43] These ascetic notions have entered Philo's thought virtually unaltered.

---

[41] Philo goes so far as to condemn those who derive pleasure from flowers. Flowers, he says in *Prov.* 2.71, "were made to give health not pleasure."

[42] Cf. *Phaedo* 67e and 64a; also see Colson's note in *PLCL* 2, 493-94.

[43] *Ibid.* p. 502.

Philo uses Plato elsewhere to add an ascetic meaning to the biblical text. In the most remarkable of these, Philo provides a Platonic gloss to the second commandment:

> The second forbids us to make gods of things which are not the causes of existence, employing for that purpose the mischievous arts of the painter and sculptor which Moses expelled from his commonwealth (*politeias*) and sentenced to perpetual banishment (*Her.* 169).

Of course the decalogue forbids the making of idols. But it was Plato, not Moses, who expelled the painter and other deceptive artists from his *politeia* (cf. *Rep.* 596ff.). In *Spec.* 1.28-29, idols are again discussed. The entire passage has Platonic overtones:

> Further, too, they have brought in sculpture and painting to co-operate in the deception, in order that with the colours and shapes and artistic qualities wrought by their fine workmanship they may enthrall the spectators and so beguile the two leading senses, sight and hearing--sight through lifeless shapes of beauty, hearing through the charm of poetry and music --and thus make the soul unsteady and unsettled and seize it for their prey (*ibid.* 29).

Since Scripture is silent on the deceptions of the arts, Philo's concern for a soul beguiled by beauty should be attributed to

Plato rather than Moses.[44]

Plato clearly played a significant role in shaping Philo's asceticism, but Plato's philosophy was not the only influence. Because Philo was involved in the practical life of his community, his asceticism has a social dimension. For however Philo dresses up his ascetic views in the mantle of philosophic abstraction, Alexandrian realities show through. And Philo's works convey the impression that a down-to-earth hatred of a life of luxury motivated him as much as a philosophical love of denial and self-restraint. For example, on the surface *Spec.* 2.18-23 is a denunciation of the life of luxury.[45] The passage begins in general terms with Philo referring to "boastful persons, of the sort that is puffed up by arrogance, who in their craving for high position determine to have nothing to do in any way with the frugal, the truly profitable mode of living" (*ibid.* 18). In the succeeding paragraph, however, Philo makes specific reference to an individual who had succumbed to the temptation of the "good" life. Philo describes him as "a man of considerable property who had found a loose and dissipated style of living to his taste" (*ibid.* 19). The object of Philo's scorn seems to be the "newly

---

[44]Cf. Winston's discussion of Wisdom 14:18-20 in his Anchor Bible edition, p. 278. Plato's aesthetic theories are not without their difficulties; cf. W.J. Verdenius, "Plato's Doctrine of Artistic Imitation" in G. Vlastos (ed.), *Plato: A Collection of Critical Essays* (2 vol.; New York, 1971), vol. 2, pp. 259-73. For a more general treatment, see J.G. Warry, *Greek Aesthetic Theory: A Study of Callistic and Aesthetic Concepts in the Works of Plato and Aristotle* (London, 1962), Ch. 3.

[45]Cf. Attridge's treatment of Josephus in *The Interpretation of Biblical History in ... Josephus*, p. 137.

rich" (*neoploutōn, ibid.* 23). It is certainly relevant to recall here that Philo belonged to a family of established wealth which might predispose him to hold the *nouveaux riches* in contempt.

Philo's denunciations of the life of luxury sometimes are prompted by passages from Scripture. For instance, on his flight to Haran, Jacob uses a stone as a pillow (Gen. 28:11). This incident provides Philo with an occasion (*Somn.* 1.120-126) to express his strong disapproval of contemporary life and morals. Philo may have been commenting on his fellow Alexandrians when he depicts lovers of luxury in the following way:

> ...these people [lovers of luxury], when they have got through their outrages upon other men in law-courts, and council-chambers, and theatres, and everywhere, come home... to ruin their own abode... I mean the body. Into it they convey an unlimited supply of eatables one after another, and steep it in quantities of strong drink, until the reasoning faculty is drowned... (*Somn.* 1.122).

Philo explicitly rejects a superficial adoption of ascetic ways, condemning those "who without full consideration give up the business and financial side of a citizen's life, and say that they have conceived a contempt for fame and pleasure" (*Fug.* 33). Hypocritical ascetics are "practising an imposture" (*ibid.*). Men should come to asceticism in the fulness of time, after devoting themselves to community service:

> Begin, then, by getting some exercise and practice in the business of life both private and public; and when by means of the sister virtues, household-management and statesmanship (*oikonomikēs te kai politikēs*), you have become masters in each domain, enter now, as more than qualified to do so, on your migration

> to a different and more excellent way of life. For the practical comes before the contemplative life; it is a sort of prelude to a more advanced contest... (*ibid*. 36).

Here Philo makes a genuine effort to balance the claims of civic responsibility against a life of ascetic withdrawal. He defends true asceticism against those who rush into it prematurely, against those who never aspire to a higher mode of life, and against those who are corrupted along the way.

Philo does not miss an opportunity to contrast the simple life with the luxurious life.[46] In *Spec*. 2.20-22, for an example, he portrays those who shun luxury. Simplicity actually improves one's material circumstances. What is more, it exalts the soul by impressing on men a sense of their common humanity. Philo thus presents asceticism not as a peculiarity of one people, but as an instance of universally approved virtue. This mode of presenting Jewish asceticism seems to be characteristic of Philo, for in discussing the dietary laws he resorts to the same sort of explanation. Moses, Philo says, did not allow the Jews full liberty in the areas of food and drink "but bridled them with ordinances most conducive to self-restraint and humanity and what is chief of all, piety" (*Spec*. 4.97). These ascetic practices establish the Jews as a people concerned with human values, a civilized nation among the nations.

To a modern reader, it must be puzzling to find in Philo an asceticism which goes beyond both Scripture and Plato. Of course we can never know all the factors which may have influenced

---

[46]Cf. *Somn*. 2.9.

Philo. But his extreme views can be explained at least in part as a response to the charges of permissiveness and lust directed against his people.

Misanthropy and Philanthropy

In antiquity both friends and foes of the Jews regarded the observance of Jewish dietary laws as an essential characteristic of the nation. Since Philo was aware that these regulations raised difficulties for some of his contemporaries, he tried to reassure them of the rationality of the laws. Philo adduced clever arguments, but there was one stubborn fact which no "modern" rationalization could alter: dietary laws in effect made it impossible for a Jew and a pagan to sit down together at the same table.[47] To pagans who were not ill disposed toward Jews, this behavior must have seemed anti-social at the very least. Thus Hecataeus[48] comments on the Jews' "unsocial and intolerant mode of life" (*apanthrōpon tina kai misoxenon bion*) even though

---

[47]Cf. *Jubilees* 22.16: "Separate thyself from the nations, do not eat with them, do not act according to their deeds, and do not associate with them, because their work is uncleanliness, all their ways contamination, detestation and abomination. They slaughter their sacrifices to the dead and pray to demons." S. Stein quotes this passage in an interesting article, "Rabbinica and Patristica on the Dietary Laws" in *Studia Patristica* (Papers presented to the Second International Conference on Patristic Studies held at Christ Church, Oxford, 1955 = *Texte und Untersuchungen zur Geschichte der altchristlichen Literatur*, vol. 64; Berlin, 1957) II, 143-47. Cf. Katz, *Exclusiveness and Tolerance*, pp. 26-27. The issue of mixing with other peoples is also mentioned in *Letter of Aristeas* 139.

[48]*GLA*, No. 11.

he is not otherwise regarded as a foe of Israel.[49] There was, in short, a social price to be paid for the dietary laws and other regulations which tended to isolate Jews from their neighbors. Yet if Philo was going to preserve his identity as a Jew, he could not repudiate certain principles. And so the stage is set for social conflict.

It has been argued that the fundamental barrier between the Jewish community and the outside world was the pagan perception of Jewish "strangeness." Sevenster has portrayed this quality in his *Roots of Pagan Anti-Semitism*. Jews, he explains, did not simply have the strangeness of an immigrant minority.

> ...the strangeness that astonished and very soon offended the people in whose midst they lived lay in their way of life and their customs, which always forced a certain degree of segregation upon them. The Jews were never quite like the others; they were always inclined to isolate themselves; they had no part in the morals and customs of the people about them, nor in that syncretism that was meant to be so tolerant. There was always something exceptional about the religion of the Jews, and this made them difficult in social intercourse, ill-adapted to the pattern of ancient society.[50]

Whether or not any particular anti-Semitic writer acknowledged it, a general perception of strangeness may have been at the heart of ancient attacks on Judaism. In order to make this abstract notion

---

[49]This point is made by Sevenster, *Roots of Pagan Anti-Semitism*, p. 89.

[50]*Idem.* For a more comprehensive view of Jewish "strangeness" see Sevenster's Ch. 3 in its entirety. Also see Daniel, "Anti-Semitism in the Hellenistic-Roman Period," p. 51.

come alive, I shall cite one classical author, Diodorus the Sicilian, who flourished during the first century b.c.e. Diodorus is cited here as an example--not because Philo was aware of him in particular, but because he presents the full range of social transgressions attributed to the Jews by their maligners.[51] Perhaps more important for our purposes, it is possible to discern in his comments an underlying sense of Jewish strangeness.[52]

According to Diodorus,

> When King Antiochus..was laying siege to Jerusalem, the Jews held out for a time, but when all their supplies were exhausted they found themselves compelled to make overtures for a cessation of hostilities. Now the majority of his friends advised the king to take the city by storm and to wipe out completely the race of Jews, since they alone of all nations avoided dealings with any other people and looked upon all men as their enemies (*Bibliotheca Historica* 34/35, 1:1).[53]

Later Diodorus says that the Jews had

---

[51]Diodorus was neither the first author to raise these issues nor the last. Compare the remarks of these authors: Posidonius (*GLA*, No. 44), Apollonius Molon (Nos. 48 and 49), Pompeius Trogus (No. 137), Damocritus (No. 247) and Tacitus (No. 281). Stern remarks (*GLA* I, 167) that Diodorus was "the least original of all known ancient historians." From our point of view, this is an asset because we are stressing the representative nature of his accusations.

[52]A.N. Sherwin-White, *Racial Prejudice in Imperial Rome* (Cambridge, 1970), p. 87.

[53]This and succeeding quotations from Diodorus may be found in *GLA*, No. 63.

> made their hatred of mankind into a tradition, and on this account had introduced utterly outlandish laws: not to break bread with any other race, nor to show them any good will at all (*ibid.* 1:2).

The villian of the piece is Moses, "founder of Jerusalem and organizer of the nation," who "ordained for the Jews their misanthropic and lawless customs." To this Diodorus immediately adds:

> And since Epiphanes was shocked by such hatred directed against all mankind, he had set himself to break down their traditional practices (*ibid.* 1:3).

Diodorus' sense of Jewish strangeness expresses itself in the claim that the Jews are misanthropes. A charge of this sort is not easy to dispel. It is not like slander in which Moses is simply misrepresented; nor is it like pagan misconceptions of particular Jewish customs. Specific claims against a Jewish hero can be corrected in an apologetic work like *De Vita Mosis*. But Diodorus' accusations are more general, and they are leveled against the Jewish community as a social group. The only way Philo could dispel these ideas was to affirm time and again the fundamental humanity of Jewish law (cf. *Spec.* 2.79), reiterating with all the vehemence he could muster that the Jews were philanthropic, humane, and open to strangers. In what follows we shall observe in some detail how Philo acknowledges and counters the charge of misanthropy.

During Philo's lifetime a group of Jewish ascetics lived in the area of the Mareotic Lake. Having retreated from the corruption of the cities, they lived contemplative lives which Philo regarded as ideal.[54] In *Cont.* 20 he describes their pursuit of solitude, explaining that they made this choice

> not from any acquired habit of misanthropical bitterness but because they know how unprofitable and mischievous are associations with persons of dissimilar character.

This passage suggests that a charge of misanthropy has been leveled against the Therapeutae. Indeed *Cont.* 20 reveals several stages of a social dialectic. That is, first the Therapeutae withdraw from human society; then either pagans or fellow Jews criticize them for their misanthropy; finally Philo takes up their cause.

This is not the only allegation of misanthropy in Philo's works. For instance in *Virt.* 141, the charge is leveled not against a small group within Judaism, but against the people as a whole:

> ...let those clever libellers continue, if they can, to accuse the nation of misanthropy and charge the laws with enjoining unsociable and unfriendly practices, when these laws so clearly extend their compassion to flocks and herds....

In *Spec.* 2.167, a similar sort of accusation appears:

> ...it astonishes me to see that some people venture to accuse of inhumanity (*apanthrōpian*) the nation which has shewn so profound a sense of fellowship and goodwill to all men everywhere, by using its prayers and festivals and first-fruit offerings as a means of supplication for the human race in general....

---

[54] Also see passages not in *Cont.* in which the contemplative life is praised (e.g., *Mig.* 47: "For what life is better than a contemplative life, or more appropriate to a rational being?").

The passages cited here are instructive because they give some indication of how Philo defends his people. First, there is the tactic of redefining terms: *i.e.*, what the critics label as "misanthropy" is really the quality of being discriminating about one's associates (*Cong.* 20). Normally, when a man withdraws from society, there are grounds for supposing he is misanthropic. But Philo reassures us that the solitude of the man of worth actually is philanthropy (*Abr.* 22-23). Second, there is the tactic of turning the tables. The Jews are not inhumane (*Spec.* 2.167). On the contrary, that quality is exhibited by other peoples[55] who, for example, regard with complacency the exposure of infants (cf. *Spec.* 3.108-11).[56] Third, there is the tactic of attributing to the Jews qualities which contradict the alleged ones. The Jews are not parochial. In fact they alone are concerned with the entire human race. Philo sets out to prove this in *Spec.* 2.167 by pointing to the universal scope of Jewish customs (seemingly unaware that some of those very customs gave rise to the charges of misanthropy in the first place). In the same spirit, Philo asserts that the "trumpet feast" has a dual significance "partly to the nation in particular, partly to all mankind in general" (*Spec.* 2.188). Likewise burnt-offerings are given "on behalf of the nation or, to speak more correctly, on behalf of the human race"

---

[55]Cf. *Mos.* 1.95 in which the Egyptians are accused of lack of humanity and impiety (*apanthrōpias kai asebeias*).

[56]Cf. *Virt.* 131-33 and Colson's note *ad loc.* Also see Winston, *Selections*, pp. 369-70, n. 428.

(*Spec.* 1.190) and the sabbath is not a festival "of a single city or country, but of the universe" (*Op.* 89).[57]

Of course Philo does not always make every stage of the social dialectic explicit. We may consider in this regard *QG* 3.62, a commentary on Gen. 17:27. No charge of misanthropy is alluded to. But the vigor with which Philo affirms the philanthropy of the Jews indicates that the context of the passage is one of contention:

> Why does Abraham circumcise those of foreign birth? The wise man is helpful and at the same time philanthropic. He saves and calls to himself not only his kinsmen and those of like opinions but also those of foreign birth and of different opinions, giving them of his own goods with patience and ascetic continence...(*QG* 3.62).

To understand the significance of this passage, we should remember that circumcision set the Jews apart from most other ancient peoples. Whether or not contemporary rabbinic authorities intended circumcision to have this effect is not at issue here.[58] What is at issue is the fact that pagans could and, as Tactitus shows (*Hist.* 5.5.2), did regard circumcision as socially divisive. From a view such as Tacitus' it is but a short step to attributing misanthropy to the Jews. In *QG* 3.62, Philo seems eager to counter this step. He argues that circumcision is not an exclusivistic rite in the private domain of xenophobic Jews.

---

[57]On the subject of Jewish philanthropy, see Winston, *The Wisdom of Solomon*, pp. 43-46.

[58]Cf. Daniel, "Anti-Semitism in the Hellenistic-Roman Period," p. 61.

Rather it is a ceremony which the philanthropic Abraham shared even with those whose opinions diverged from his own. Circumcision thus becomes the means by which a Jewish sage teaches continence to foreigners.

In some instances, especially those connected with sexual morality, Philo offers a severe interpretation of Scripture.[59] At the same time, in his attempt to portray the Jewish nation as humane and philanthropic, Philo often adopts a more lenient stance toward the Bible. Nowhere is this better, or more appropriately, illustrated than in his presentation of the laws concerning war. Deut. 20:10-11 states that an enemy which agrees to an offer of peace should be made subject to the children of Israel. An enemy which refuses is to receive the full measure of Israelite wrath: men are to be put to the sword; women, children, and cattle are to be taken as spoil (*ibid.* 12-14). When Philo deals with the same contingencies, he deliberately chooses a more charitable course:

> ...if they [the enemy] yield they may obtain the supreme boon of friendship, but if they refuse to listen and continue their opposition, you may with justice to reinforce you advance to defend yourselves in the hope of victory (*Virt.* 109).

Philo again moderates a biblical account when he discusses women captured in war (Deut. 21:10-14). In this instance, Philo adds a passage which has no parallel in Scripture:

> ...do not treat her as a captive, and vent your passion on her, but in a gentler spirit pity her

---

[59]I refer to Philo's views on the treatment of prostitutes, *etc.*; see *supra*, p. 94.

> for her change of lot and alleviate her misfortunes by changing her condition for the better in every way (*Virt.* 110).

It should not be thought that Philo always had to alter or amend Scripture in order to prove his point. The Bible itself provided him a wealth of evidence for the humanity (*philanthrōpia*)[60] of the Jews. Moses exemplifies this quality most clearly. Actually Philo sees Moses as suffering from a handicap, for "Greek men of letters have refused to treat him as worthy of memory..." (*Mos.* 1.2). Philo continues,

> Most of these authors have abused the powers which education gave them, by composing in verse or prose comedies and pieces of voluptuous licence... when they should have used their natural gifts to the full on the lessons taught by good men and their lives (*ibid.* 3).

Philo's perception is not wide of the mark. For instance, in a passage already cited, Diodorus charged that Moses "ordained for the Jews their misanthropic and lawless customs" (*Bibliotheca Historica* 34/35, 1:3).[61] Is it any wonder that Philo should attempt to rehabilitate Moses by affirming his *philanthrōpia*? Among Moses' virtues, pride of place goes to that quality (*Mos.*

---

[60]For the range of meanings of this word, see Colson's note, *PLCL* 8, 194-95.

[61]See *supra*, pp. 105f. On Moses' alleged misanthropy, see J.G. Gager, *Moses in Greco-Roman Paganism* (SBL Monograph Series, 16; Nashville, 1972), pp. 86f., and M. Radin, *The Jews among the Greeks and Romans* (Philadelphia, 1915), p. 182.

2.9). Indeed, as we read in *Virt.* 51, Moses loved *philanthrōpia* "more than anyone else has done."

The ordinances of Scripture, as formulated by Moses, are models of humanity. The most extensive treatment of this theme may be found in *Virt.* 82-101. Elsewhere Philo praises the *philanthrōpia* of the laws concerning the sabbatical year (*Hypoth.* 7.18-19)[62] and the practice of releasing a Jewish slave after six years of servitude (*Spec.* 2.79-81).[63] The latter example, applying specifically to a Jewish slave, raises an interesting problem.

Many of the laws in which Philo takes an understandable pride seem to have been written by a Jewish legislator for the exclusive benefit of his fellow-countrymen (cf. *Virt.* 101). Philo was cosmopolitan enough to realize the weakness in this; he knew that a detractor of the Jews could charge that the concept of *philanthrōpia* should apply universally. Consequently Philo attempts to expand the notion, first by including proselytes:

> Having laid down laws for members of the same nation, he [Moses] holds that the incomers (*epēlutas*) too should be accorded every favour and consideration as their due.... He commands all members of the nation to love the incomers (*epēlutas*), not only as friends and kinsfolk but as themselves (*Virt.* 102-103).

Philo then applies the concept to non-Jewish settlers (*metoikoi* in *Virt.* 105) and later to the (hypothetical?) case of Egyptians who "wish to pass over into the Jewish community." Of the latter, he writes:

---

[62]Cf. *Spec.* 2.86-109; *Virt.* 97-98.

[63]Cf. *Spec.* 4.15.

> ...they must not be spurned with an unconditional refusal as children of enemies, but be so far favoured that the third generation is invited to the congregation and made partakers in the divine revelations, to which also the native born, whose lineage is beyond reproach, are rightfully admitted (*ibid*. 108).

The passages from *De Virtutibus* which relate to *philanthrōpia* are of prime importance for our understanding of Philo. For that concept, as it gradually unfolds, is an indication of the limits of the spiritual community in which Philo was ideally prepared to participate. Philo seems to recognize that *philanthrōpia* does not apply exclusively to one's closest associates; the concept itself has a centrifugal force. In this, Philo may have been influenced by an idea of universalism in which all men are ultimately linked (*Spec*. 1.211) and in which Jews have a unique role to play (*ibid*. 97). Whatever moved him, his use of the concept of *philanthrōpia* indicates that on one level he made an effort to broaden his human sympathies.

But even as Philo proclaims the openness of the Jews to other peoples, we can detect a counter-current of exclusiveness which undermines the very concept he espouses. When Joseph's brothers come down to Egypt, Joseph says that he will make peace partly because of "the natural humanity (*tē physikē philanthrōpia*) which I feel to all men, and particularly to those of my blood" (*Jos*. 240). This formulation is a fair rendition of Gen. 45:3ff. It is also indicative of a quandary: how does Philo balance the universal claims of *philanthrōpia* with a very specific commitment to Judaism?

V. DRAWING THE LINE

A People Apart

In a poignant passage, Philo says that "the whole Jewish race is in the position of an orphan compared with all the nations on every side" (*Spec.* 4.179). When misfortunes befall other nations, allies come to their aid; not so with the Jews:

> ... the Jewish nation has none to take its part, as it lives under exceptional laws which are necessarily grave and severe, because they inculcate the highest standard of virtue. But gravity is austere, and austerity is held in aversion by the great mass of men because they favour pleasure (*ibid.*).

With the gift of hindsight, *Spec.* 4.179 appears ominously prophetic. It is not our purpose to reflect on how history has borne out the truth of Philo's comments. Our purpose is rather to consider this passage as evidence of Philo's social perception--an expression of one man's assessment of the relations between Jews and their neighbors.

What Philo stresses in *Spec.* 4.179 is a strong sense of Jewish isolation.[1] Philo believed that the pagans were ultimately responsible for this condition. In his view, the Jews were the innocent victims of their pleasure-seeking neighbors. Although we cannot doubt Philo's subjective impressions, in all fairness we should remember that Philo called for the Jews to separate

---

[1] Physically, Alexandrian Jews do not appear to have been isolated. As Philo attests in *Flac.* 55, Alexandrian Jews lived in specific quarters of the city. The consensus of scholarly opinion is that the Jews themselves created this demographic condition. Cf. V.A. Tcherikover, *et al.*, *Corpus Papyrorum Judaicarum* (3 vols.; Cambridge, 1957-64) I, 5-6.

themselves from their pagan neighbors. In a passage already quoted at greater length,[2] Philo warned his brethren not to "fraternize with the multitude, resort to their temples...[or] join in their libations and sacrifices" (*Spec.* 1.316). Anyone who suggests that a Jew should do these things must be punished "as a public and general enemy" (*ibid.*). The threat of polytheism undoubtedly was in Philo's mind when he made this statement. But Philo's pagan neighbors may not have appreciated the full range of inferences which Philo and his co-religionists drew from the initial premise of monotheism.

Philo's attempt to separate Jew from pagan in *Spec.* 4.179 raises an important question: how did Philo see the other peoples who lived around him? For if we assume that pagan hostility did not descend upon the Jewish world "out of the blue"--that is, if we allow for the existence of antecedent determining factors--then we must study Philo's attitudes to both Egyptians and Greeks.

The Egyptians

Egyptians and their objects of worship are often ridiculed in the works of Philo. The following passage may be taken as representative:

> ...as for the gods of the Egyptians it is hardly decent even to mention them. The Egyptians have promoted to divine honours irrational

---

[2]Cf. *supra*, p. 34.

> animals, not only of the tame sort but also beasts of the utmost savagery...(*Cont.* 8).³

In Philo's view, the character of men and nations was reflected in their gods. The Egyptians therefore condemned themselves when they deified the most savage creatures in the universe. As Philo remarks in *Legat.* 166, the venom and temper of crocodiles and asps were reproduced in the Egyptian soul.

In keeping with the unholy Egyptian pantheon, Egypt represents the lowest elements Philo can imagine for his allegories. Egypt is body (e.g., *Cong.* 20-21; *Conf.* 70; *Agr.* 88-89; *Sac.* 130; *Ebr.* 95), pleasure (e.g., *Fug.* 147f; *QG* 4.177), atheism (e.g., *Post.* 2; *Fug.* 180), and passion (e.g., *Cong.* 83-85; *LA* 2.103; *Mig.* 202). Furthermore, Egyptians are jealous (*Flac.* 29) and arrogant by nature (*Agr.* 62). Several characteristics alleged by Philo warrant special attention. In *Mos.* 1.95, he speaks of the inhumanity and impiety (*apanthrōpias kai asebeias*) of the Egyptians.⁴ In *Abr.* 107 he refers to their inhospitality and licentiousness (*axenon kai akolaston*).⁵ These last four charges against the Egyptians are of particular interest because the same allegations--often in the same words--were made against the Jews. Philo has simply turned the tables, shifting the target of calumny

---

³Cf. Winston's discussion of Wisdom 15:14-19 in his Anchor Bible edition, pp. 289-91.

⁴Cf. *QE* 1.10: "He [God] judged all the Egyptians to be equally impious, unworthy and unclean"; also see *ibid.* 18.

⁵Philo repeats the charge of licentiousness in *Post.* 156.

from his own people to the one group which was lower down on the social scale.

According to Philo, Egyptians had an "ancient and we might say innate hostility to the Jews" (*Flac.* 29). Perhaps because of the long-standing nature of the conflict, Philo did not attempt to elucidate the phenomenon to his contemporaries. As Philo presents it, Egyptian hostility was gratuitous and its cause (if indeed there was one) was lost in time. Two factors are noteworthy here: the ease with which Philo transfers malicious allegations from the Jews to the Egyptians and the pleasure in paradox which he conveys when he points out that the Israelite slaves in Egypt were better than the Egyptians who enslaved them (*Conf.* 91). These factors suggest that the hostility was reciprocal.[6]

That Philo did little to ameliorate the situation is evident from his treatment of various passages from Scripture. If we compare, for instance, Philo's version of the Golden Calf (*Mos.* 2.161-62, 270) with the biblical account (Exod. 32:1-24),[7] it is clear that Philo added anti-Egyptian elements which were not justified by the text. From an Egyptian point of view, no good will is evident in Philo's reference to Hagar (*Abr.* 251; cf. Gen.

---

[6] A similar turning of the tables may be discerned in *Cher.* 96. The votaries of pagan rites are diseased and mutilated, not the Jews. Cf. the view of Lysimachus that the Jews were diseased (Josephus, *Apion.* 1. 304-11 = *GLA*, No. 158). Also see the view of Apion (*Apion.* 2. 15-28 = *GLA*, No. 165).

[7] Cf. Colson's note in *PLCL* 6, 528.

16:1).[8] Nor does a desire for reconciliation characterize his discussion of Joseph's sovereignty over the land of Egypt (*Jos.* 119-21; cf. Gen. 41:39ff.) or his accounts of Moses killing the Egyptian (*Mos.* 1.44 and *LA* 3.37-39; cf. Exod. 2:11-15). In some of these passages, Philo may actually follow the lead of Scripture. But an accomplished allegorist could easily have smoothed over any reference which reflected ill on the Egyptians if he had wanted to bring about rapprochment between Egyptian and Jew.[9]

Even though Philo does not attempt to placate the Egyptians as a nation, he does endeavor to explain those events in the common history of the Jews and Egyptians which might reflect poorly on the Jews as a guest people. Anyone acquainted with the Bible would know that the Hebrews left Egypt, both literally and figuratively, under a cloud.[10] Scripture itself mentions that they took spoil with them (Exod. 12:35-36). Because of this, Philo

---

[8]See Sandmel, *Philo's Place*, pp. 135-36.

[9]Does Philo ever say anything positive about the Egyptians? Surprisingly, the answer to this question is yes. In *Spec.* 1.2, Philo refers to the Egyptian race "as pre-eminent for its populousness, its antiquity and its attachment to philosophy." Of course, in each of these categories, the Jews will prove to be equal or superior to the Egyptians. But let it be recorded here that not every Philonic reference to the Egyptians is negative.

[10]Cf. J.W. Parkes, *The Conflict of the Church and the Synagogue: A Study in the Origins of Antisemitism* (London, 1934), pp. 15-16.

adopts an apologetic stance. His people did not plunder the Egyptians "in avarice, or, as their accusers might say, in covetousness of what belonged to others." Philo's own explanation follows:

> In the first place, they were but receiving a bare wage for all their time of service; secondly, they were retaliating, not on an equal but on a lesser scale, for their enslavement (*Mos.* 1.141).[11]

The Hebrews had originally migrated to Egypt "through lack of food.... They were, in a sense, suppliants, who had found a sanctuary in the pledged faith of the king and the pity felt for them by the inhabitants" (*ibid.* 34). The Jews knew the rules governing the behavior of suppliants: Joseph's conduct with the wife of Potiphar (*Jos.* 40-48) exemplified for Philo the behavior expected of those on whom hospitality is bestowed.[12] The Egyptians, however, did not know their roles as protectors of strangers:

> In thus making serfs of men who were not only free but guests, suppliants and settlers (*xenous kai hiketas kai metoikous*), he showed no shame or fear of the God of liberty and hospitality

---

[11] The reader will observe here the echoes of a debate. Philo is not defending his people in a vacuum; real charges have been made and Philo is answering those charges. See Winston, *Selections*, p. 389, n. 679. Also see the same author's excellent notes in the Anchor Bible edition of Wisdom 10:15-21 (pp. 219-23).

[12] In *Jos.* 216, Philo says that injuring a benefactor is "a most unholy deed."

and of justice to guests and suppliants... (*Mos.* 1.36).[13]

Because Philo perceived the Jewish nation surrounded by actual or potential enemies, it was crucial for him to depict the Jews as scrupulous and fair-minded in dealing with others, even their enemies (cf. *Spec.* 4.224). Philo's concern in these passages was not to improve relations with contemporary Egyptians. Rather it was to reassure the authorities that the Jews were reliable citizens.

Since Egyptians were at the bottom of the social ladder, the hellenized Jews of Alexandria may have thought that they could dismiss them with impunity. After all, who would champion their cause? Philo certainly did not scruple to treat them with contempt. This may have been a miscalculation, for the Egyptians provided much of the brawn which was directed against the Jews in the pogrom of the year 38 c.e.[14] As for the cause of that hostility, Philo's explanation of this phenomenon solely in terms of the Egyptian national character (*Flac.* 29) is too facile, especially in view of the anti-Egyptian rhetoric which permeates his own work. Philo slips with such ease into passages which defame Egypt, its people, and its religion that one wonders how

---

[13] On the subject of enslaving guests, see Winston's discussion of Wisdom 19:13-14 in the Anchor Bible edition, pp. 327-29.

[14] Exploited by the Romans financially and manipulated by the Greeks of Alexandria for their own political purposes, the Egyptians ended up playing conspicuous roles in a pogrom which they had not created. Cf. A. Segrè, "Antisemitism in Hellenistic Alexandria," *Jewish Social Studies* 8 (1946), 133.

common this mode of thought was within the Jewish community. Indeed if Alexandrian Jews thought in this way about things Egyptian, perhaps we should reassess the assumption that the Jews played no part in the deterioration of relations between the peoples. The Egyptians may not actually have read Philo's works. But since attitudes are disseminated more easily than treatises, his views may have colored the atmosphere.

The Greeks

Whereas Egyptians and Jews coexisted in a state of mutual hatred and suspicion, the situation was quite different between Greeks and their hellenized Jewish neighbors. In Philo's circle, Greeks were admired--even envied--for the richness of their cultural legacy and for their aristocratic pretensions. Although distrustful of Jews who acquired a veneer of Greek culture in order to improve their social standing, Philo could not disapprove of co-religionists who had a genuine interest in Greek education.[15] Philo himself had successfully integrated Greek thought into his Jewish life, and his attitude toward the pagan bearers of Greek tradition was positive.

And yet Philo was aware that certain influential Greeks did not return his warm sentiments. In *Flac.* 20, Philo mentions three Greeks, Dionysius, Lampo, and Isidorus, who were confidants of Flaccus, the Roman prefect of Egypt. Flaccus should have rejected these miscreants "as sedition-makers and enemies of the commonwealth..." (*Flac.* 24). Instead he took their advice which

---

[15]See my *SEPA*, p. 30.

was inimical to the welfare of the city's Jews. Interestingly enough, these same characters reappear in sources outside the Philonic corpus. A careful analysis of these sources provides us with an insight into their political views and motivations.[16] Representing Greek nationalistic interests in Alexandria, they were the prime movers behind the pogrom of 38 c.e. Philo never explicitly accuses Greeks of acting as a group with malicious intent toward Jews. Yet undoubtedly he was conscious of their hostility and the ways in which they expressed it.

In order to understand Greek attitudes, it would be appropriate to give a sketch of Graeco-Jewish relations prior to the Alexandrian pogrom. Before the year 30 b.c.e., apparently relations between Greeks and Jews were not particularly strained. Then came the great divide: the Jews supported the victorious Romans in Egypt. From the Jewish point of view there could be no real choice between Rome and a Greek *polis* (with all the religious practices which a *polis* implied). As Tcherikover has noted,

---

[16]See the collection of semi-literary fragments edited by Herbert A. Musurillo, under the title *The Acts of the Pagan Martyrs: Acta Alexandrinorum* (Oxford, 1954). This collection allows us to gain a deeper insight into the political dynamics of the pogrom of 38. One comment by Musurillo is significant in this regard, for it indicates the class of Alexandrian Greek with which Philo was dealing. "In reading through the *Acta,* one is struck by the recurrence of the names of men... [from the] gymnasiarch class: Isidorus, Lampon, Theon, Dionysius, Appian--all men who filled Alexandria's highest magistracies, were perhaps members of the *gerousia,* and often acted as Alexandria's representatives at the imperial court" (p. 273).

> The Jewish communities in Egypt (and Alexandria was no exception to the rule) were dependent upon the central government, and the stronger this government was, the better it was for the Jews. It would have been a calamity for the Jewish *politeuma* of Alexandria had it been dependent upon the decisions of the Greek *polis*, and not on the more or less impartial orders of the central government. When the Jews had to choose between Alexandria and Rome, they chose Rome.[17]

When we recall the commercial rivalry between Alexandria and Rome, we can well understand that from the point of view of Alexandrian Greeks the Jews had "betrayed the national cause of Egypt."[18]

Perhaps as a result of Jewish opposition to Cleopatra, the conquering Octavian was very sensitive to the privileges which Jews had enjoyed within his realm. The Jews, however, far from acting the part of an unobtrusive guest-people, *demanded* of the emperor "that they should not be forced to desecrate the Sabbath, that they be exempted from military service and from the associated taxes, that ... liturgies should not be levied from them, and that they be permitted to collect money and send it to Jerusalem."[19] And the emperor responded by confirming the Jews in all their former privileges.

Apparently two Jewish privileges were particularly irksome to the Alexandrian Greek population: the collection of the Jerusalem

---

[17]Tcherikover, *CPJ* I, 56.

[18]*Ibid.* p. 55.

[19]Tcherikover, *Hellenistic Civilization*, p. 373.

Drawing the Line 125

tax and the existence of a Jewish *gerousia*. With regard to the first it should be noted that attempts were made under Augustus to halt the shipping of sacred dues (gold) out of the country. But the Jews complained and this traditional privilege--financial drain though it was--was reaffirmed.[20] The question of the Jewish *gerousia*, however, is somewhat more complicated.

The *gerousia* was the official governing body of the Jewish *politeuma*. Because the Jewish community was actually subject to Graeco-Egyptian law, the jurisdiction of the seventy-one-member *gerousia* was limited to matters involving religious life and practice.[21] Yet its very existence became a source of conflict between the Greek and Jewish communities from the time of the Roman conquest. For while Augustus was reaffirming Jewish privileges, including the *gerousia*[22], he was refusing the citizens of Alexandria the senate which they had demanded. And even though the Jewish communal authorities had little (if anything) to say in questions of civil government, it was a sore point among the Greeks whose nationalism increased as Alexandria herself was

---

[20] Segrè, "The Status of the Jews in Ptolemaic and Roman Egypt," *Jewish Social Studies* 6 (1944), 394. Also see *GLA*, No. 68 and Stern's notes, esp. I, 198-99; and Smallwood's edition of Philo's treatise *Legatio*, p. 238.

[21] In this paragraph I am indebted to Segrè, "The Status of the Jews in Ptolemaic and Roman Egypt," p. 389. Also see Smallwood, *Legatio*, pp. 3-14 and *passim*.

[22] See Stern's view that the *gerousia* was strengthened, *GLA*, I, 280-81. Also see *idem*, pp. 398-403.

reduced "from a royal residence and head of a sovereign state to a mere provincial capital."[23]

Another source of conflict between Greeks and Jews may be traced back to the decision of Rome to impose a poll-tax (known as the *laographia*) upon the Jews. The imposition of *laographia* was in Jewish eyes "not merely an additional expense but also a mark of extreme political and cultural degradation, putting them on the same level with the Egyptian fellahin.... The only way of avoiding the unpleasant situation created by the introduction of the poll-tax ... was to obtain Alexandrian citizenship."[24] Since the main way of obtaining civic rights in Alexandria was to enroll in a Greek gymnasium, the Jews increasingly turned to those institutions in their struggle for emancipation and equality with the Greeks. The latter, however, feeling with good reason that the traditional form of the *polis* was being threatened, had the doors of their gymnasia closed to outsiders.[25]

Having surveyed some of the political issues which provoked hostility from the Greek camp, we shall now turn to Philo's perception of the Greeks. A most telling passage in this regard is *Flac.* 49-50, which purports to be an address by the beleaguered Jews of Alexandria to their Greek enemies. The Jews reproach the Greeks in these words:

---

[23] H.I. Bell, "Anti-semitism in Alexandria," *Journal of Roman Studies*, 31 (1941), 4.

[24] Tcherikover, *CPJ* I, 61.

[25] See the letter of Claudius to the Alexandrians, lines 90-93 (=*CPJ*, No. 153, esp. Tcherikover's notes, II, p. 53).

> You have failed to see that you are not adding to but taking from the honour given to our masters, and you do not understand that everywhere in the habitable world the religious veneration of the Jews for the Augustan house has its basis as all may see in the meeting-houses (*proseuchai*), and if we have these destroyed no place, no method is left to us for paying this homage (*Flac.* 49).

What is remarkable about this passage is the suggestion that the Greeks should reassess their position so as to take into account the interests of Rome. Philo assumes that if only the Greeks realized that they were diminishing the prestige of Rome, they would call a halt to their anti-Semitic activities. This speech might strike a modern reader as hopelessly naive. First of all, the favored position of the Jews vis-à-vis Rome did nothing but irritate the Greeks. Then the Greeks had no reason whatsoever to promote the interests of Rome. On the contrary, modern research has shown that the Greeks sought to undermine the interests of Rome.[26] In all this, Philo appears to be oblivious to a basic truth: Jews could not show deference to Rome and, at the same time, expect to maintain cordial relations with Greeks whose *polis* Rome had effectively destroyed.

Despite appearances, Philo was neither naive nor oblivious to real politics. His attempt in *Flac.* 49-50 to create a common interest between Greeks and Jews is not a practical call to action; it is more an instance of wishful thinking, an expression of his desire for rapprochement with the one alien sector of the population whose accomplishments he respected. *Flac.* 49-50 is

---

[26]Cf. Bell, "Anti-semitism in Alexandria," pp. 4-5.

Philo's response to a most disturbing incongruity: the Greeks whom he admired for their cultural attainments were (at least in Alexandria) irreconcilably opposed to his people. While avoiding the extremes of total religious withdrawal from secular society on the one hand and assimilation on the other, Philo hoped to find a comfortable middle ground on which Jews could live in peace with their Greek neighbors. Such a community would have been based on mutual respect and, as Philo points out so often, on continued observance of ancestral customs.

Jewish Virtue; or, the Spiritual Supremacy of the Jews

From the available evidence, it appears that the hostility between Jews and pagans moved in both directions and was kept alive by a dynamic interplay of forces. Nevertheless in passages like *Spec.* 4.179,[27] Philo gives the impression that the hostility originated with the pagans and was caused by pagan awareness of the high standard of Jewish virtue. Since the picture is more complicated than this, we shall assess Philo's sense of the superiority of the Jews and then see what implications it may have had for a pagan.

Philo's concept of the superiority of the Jews may be gleaned from three passages in *De Specialibus Legibus*:

> Among the other nations the priests are accustomed to offer prayers and sacrifices for their kinsmen and friends and fellow-countrymen only, but the high priest of the Jews makes prayers and gives thanks not only on behalf of the whole human race but also for

---

[27]Cf. *supra*, p. 115.

> the parts of nature, earth, water, air, fire, (1.97).
>
> [Moses] did not permit his people to conduct their festivities like other nations, but first he bade them in the very hour of their joy make themselves pure by curbing the appetites for pleasure (1.193).
>
> The Jewish nation is to the whole inhabited world what the priest is to the State (2.163).

In each of these passages, Philo acclaims the virtues of the Jews and, at the same time, manages to denigrate some aspect of paganism. One recurrent theme in Philo's essays in comparative anthropology is the spiritual supremacy of the Jews, a conclusion he draws from virtually every aspect of Jewish life.

The assumptions underlying Philo's attitudes are straightforward. In Philo's view, there could be no agreement between Jew and pagan on the question of what was sacred (cf. *Agr.* 112-19). Egyptians, for instance, were not to touch even the remains of a Jewish sacrifice because their hands were "unworthy and unclean" (*QE* 1.18). Under no conditions could paganism influence Judaism. Yet Philo proudly asserts that the Jews influenced other nations:

> ...not only Jews but almost every other people, particularly those which take more account of virtue, have so far grown in holiness as to value and honour our laws.... We may fairly say that mankind from east to west, every country and nation and state, shew aversion to foreign institutions, and think that they will enhance the respect for their own by shewing disrespect for those of other countries. It is

> not so with ours. They attract and win the attention of all, of barbarians, of Greeks, of dwellers on the mainland and islands, of nations of the east and the west, of Europe and Asia, of the whole inhabited world from end to end (*Mos.* 2.17-20).

Philo goes on to comment on the universal esteem accorded to the sabbath (*ibid.* 21-22) and the Day of Atonement (*ibid.* 23-24), concluding with the observation that "the sanctity of our legislation has been a source of wonder not only to the Jews but also to all other nations" (*ibid.* 25). The historical accuracy of Philo's remarks is not at issue here; our concern is with the import of Philo's perceptions.

According to Philo, the Torah differed from the law of other nations in that it was given by God to the Jews who carry a likeness of the commandments "enshrined in their souls" (*Legat.* 210). Because Jews bear within themselves the standard against which all acts are measured, openness to external influence is not a real option.[28] By subscribing to laws which did not provide for genuine mutuality between nations, the Jews further intensified their own isolation. In general, Philo's attitude toward pagan religion is condescending and dismissive. Ultimately the Jews will exercise hegemony over the world, as Philo writes in *Mos.* 2.44:

> ... if a fresh start should be made to brighter prospects, how great a change for the better might we expect to see! I believe that each nation would abandon its peculiar ways, and,

---

[28] Daniel, "Anti-Semitism in the Hellenistic-Roman Period," points out that "Judaism stood out as an intolerant religion in a society which was generally tolerant toward divergent beliefs" (pp. 60-61).

> throwing overboard its ancestral customs, turn
> to honouring our laws alone.

In the meantime, Philo regarded the spiritual supremacy of his nation as a fact of life.

As noted earlier, Philo utilizes many aspects of Jewish life to demonstrate the spiritual supremacy of the Jews and the spiritual inadequacy, if not inferiority, of the pagans. In making his cross-cultural observations, Philo relies on two elements. The first is a strong sense for the differences between his people and the peoples around him. This is evident in *Flac.* 43:

> What then did the governor of the country do? He knew that both Alexandria and the whole of Egypt had two kinds of inhabitants, us and them, and that there were no less than a million Jews resident in Alexandria and the country from the slope into Libya to the boundaries of Ethiopia; also that this was an attack against them all....

The issue being discussed here is a political or strategic one, but behind it lies Philo's perception of a world cleft in two. The second feature of Philo's cross-cultural observations is his implicit recognition of certain *similarities* between pagan and Jewish customs. That is to say, when Philo contrasts religious practices he is not contrasting utterly different things. Indeed, an unbiased observer, witnessing Jewish sacrifices alongside pagan ones, might be tempted to classify them under the same heading.[29] This is precisely the problem. To preserve his sense of Jewish exclusiveness, Philo tells his audience that Jewish sacrifice and

---

[29] On the alleged link between Dionysiac and Jewish cults, see Plutarch, *Quaestiones Convivales* 671 D-672B (= *GLA*, No. 258).

pagan sacrifice are worlds apart. *Our* (Jewish) sacrifices, he would say, are actually not at all the same as *their* (pagan) sacrifices. By stressing differences, in the face of superficial similarities, Philo sets his people apart and, in the process, gives expression to the Jews' sense of uniqueness.

Since I have used the example of sacrifice, let us see how Philo actually deals with that subject in its most extreme form. The Akedah, or binding of Isaac, provides a perfect illustration of how Philo asserts his identity by contrast with other peoples. Philo was well aware that there were instances of child-sacrifice among the nations. This fact provided him with a challenge: he had to prove the distinctivenss of the Jewish event. Philo first turns to certain unnamed critics[30] who "misconstrue everything," arguing that Abraham's action was neither great nor wonderful "as we suppose it to be" (*Abr.* 178). These critics insist that

> ...many other persons, full of love for their kinsfolk and offspring, have given their children, some to be sacrificed for their country to serve as a price to redeem it from wars or drought or excessive rainfall or pestilence, others for the sake of what was held to be piety though it is not really so. Indeed they say that among the Greeks men of the highest reputation, not only private individuals but kings, have with little thought of their offspring put them to death... (*Abr.* 179-180).

If these claims were allowed to go unchallenged, Judaism would be deprived of a distinctive moment in history. Since such a critique made Jewish and pagan sacrifice appear morally equivalent, Philo

---

[30]For Sandmel's ideas regarding the identity of these detractors, see *Philo's Place*, p. 128.

did all he could to destroy this erroneous impression. For instance in *Abr.* 184, he writes:

> Some of those who sacrifice their children follow custom in so doing, as was the case according to the critics with some of the barbarians. Others have important and painful reasons for their action because their cities and countries cannot but fail otherwise. These give their children partly under compulsion and the pressure of higher powers, partly through desire for glory and honour, to win fame at the time and a good name in the future.

In subsequent passages (*Abr.* 185-93), Philo endeavors to show that Abraham was not moved by such ignoble considerations. On the general question of child-sacrifice, Philo dissociates himself from the barbarians who practiced it:

> So if we are victorious over our enemies, let us not affect their impious ways in which they think to show their piety by burning their sons and daughters to their gods (*Spec.* 1.312).

In the end, Philo denies even the humanity of Isaac (*Abr.* 194; cf. *Mig.* 140), thereby removing the source of debate on child-sacrifice within Judaism. The divorce between Judaism and paganism on this issue thus is complete.

In *Spec.* 1.162-256, Philo sets forth in elaborate detail the biblical regulations for animal sacrifice. The sheer length of his discussion raises a question: why should Philo have been concerned with issues which could have had only a marginal practical relevance for him? After all, Philo himself was not an inverterate pilgrim to Jerusalem, and, given the opportunity, he tended to spiritualize sacrifice. In my view, he wrote this section at least in part to demonstrate that the sacrifices of the Jews differed fundamentally from those of pagans. By presenting Jewish sacrifice in all its distinctive detail, Philo once again sets off the Jews as a people apart.

When Philo concludes one of his expositions on proper sacrifice, he makes a significant remark: "That what I have said above is true and is the word not of myself but of nature is attested not only by its self-evident certitude... but also by the law..." (*Spec.* 1.273). It is not surprising, then, that when pagan and Jewish customs are contrasted, Jewish ritual emerges triumphant. This result is virtually guaranteed by Philo's belief that the Torah epitomized the law of nature (cf. *Op.* 3). Philo seems to have regarded with contempt those who did not carry the true standard of Torah in their souls:

> The virtues have their conception and their birthpangs, but when I purpose to speak of them let them who corrupt religion into superstition close their ears or depart. For this is a divine mystery and its lesson is for the initiated.... The sacred revelation is not for those others who, under the spell of the deadly curse of vanity, have no other standards for measuring what is pure and holy but their barren words and phrases and their silly usages and ritual (*Cher.* 42).

Bearing in mind Philo's belief that the Torah was the standard of all things, we may take note of other Jewish-pagan contrasts which appear in his works. In each case, paganism is placed in the dock and is explicitly found wanting.

(1) *Banquets*. Philo recalls two celebrated Greek banquets: that of Xenophon characterized by "unrestrained merrymaking" (*Cont.* 58) and that of Plato characterized by talk of "vulgar

love" (*pandēmos erōs*, *Cont.* 60). Philo compares these symposia with similar occasions of the Therapeutae. The Greek ones "appear as matters for derision" (*ibid.* 58). Elsewhere Philo adds, "the disciples of Moses trained from their earliest years to love the truth regard them with supreme contempt and continue undeceived" (*ibid.* 63; also see *ibid.* 64). A similar dichotomy may be found in "the modern [pagan] way of taking strong drink" as opposed to the ancient Jewish way (*Plant.* 160-64).

(2) *Female chastity.* Some Greek priestesses remained chaste only under compulsion. Jewish women among the Therapeutae were chaste "of their own free will in their ardent yearning for wisdom" (*Cont.* 68).

(3) *Mourning.* The customs observed by Abraham while in mourning showed the patriarch to be morally superior to his neighbors:

> Now, when the chief men of the country came to sympathize and saw nothing of the sort of mourning which was customary with themselves, no wailing, no chanting of dirges, no beating of breasts either of men or of women, but a quiet sober air of sorrow pervading the whole house, they were profoundly amazed... (*Abr.* 260).

Abraham's self-restraint indicates a higher state of spiritual development.

(4) *The lawgiver.* Philo was aware of at least two pagan models of lawgiving (cf. *Op.* 1-3). Moses deliberately rejected both of these models, refraining "on the one hand, from stating abruptly what should be practised or avoided, and on the other hand...from inventing myths himself or acquiescing in those composed by others" (*Op.* 2). Consequently, Philo could say of

Moses that he was "the best of all lawgivers in all countries, better in fact than any that have ever arisen among either the Greeks or the barbarians..."(*Mos.* 2.12).

(5) *Myths.* In *Conf.* 2, Philo has an impious scoffer issue the following challenge, presumably to a believing Jew:

> Can you still speak gravely of the ordinances as containing the canons of absolute truth? For see your so-called holy books contain also myths (*mythous*), which you regularly deride when you hear them related by others.

How does Philo explain the close parallels between Scripture and the works of pagan mythographers (*Conf.* 6)? First of all, he denies the charge: "God is an author in whose works you will find no myth" (*mythou men plasma ouden, Det.* 125). Poets and sophists delight in myths; Scripture does not present us with myth at all, but rather with ideas made visible (*Op.* 157). The difference between an account from Scripture and a pagan myth bearing some superficial resemblance to it lies in the fact that only the biblical one points to a higher reality. Pagan myths then are false, mere artifacts of man. This is made explicit in Philo's treatment of the verse (Gen. 6:14) which states that there were giants on the earth:

> Some may think that the Lawgiver is alluding to the myths of the poets about the giants, but indeed myth-making is a thing most alien to him, and his mind is set on following in the steps of truth.... And therefore also he has banished from his own commonwealth (*politeias*) painting and sculpture... because their crafts belie the nature of truth and work deception and illusions through the eyes to souls that are ready to be seduced. So, then,

> it is no myth at all of giants that he sets before us... (*Gig.* 58-60).

Here Philo begins his allegorical interpretation. The reader should note that in this passage pagan myths are relegated to a Platonic limbo along with other works of illusion.[31] From Philo, who takes metaphysics seriously, this is a sign of contempt.

(6) *Festivals.* In his treatise *De Cherubim*, Philo contrasts the observance of Jewish and pagan festivals. In describing the festal assemblies of the pagans, Philo again invokes the language of myth:

> Different nations, whether Greek or barbarian, have their own [festivals], the product of myth and fiction (*ek mythikōn plasmatōn*), and their only purpose is empty vanity. We need not dwell on them, for the whole of human life would not suffice to tell in detail of the follies inherent in them (*Cher.* 91).

At this point Philo offers his readers a most unflattering sketch of pagan festivals (*ibid.* 91-97); in them every vice and sacrilege may be found. "Such are the feasts," Philo says, "of those whom men call happy" (*ibid.* 94). True happiness, it is clear, lies with the Jews whose festivals exemplify every virtue.[32]

Thus many spheres of life provided Philo with the occasion to draw explicit contrasts between Judaism and paganism. As a Jewish sage said, *Kol ma'aseihem shel Yisra'el muvdalim*

---

[31] The concept of myth in Philo does not apply exclusively to pagan stories. For instance, in *LA* 2.19, Philo rejects the literal meaning of Gen. 2:21: "These words in their literal sense are of the nature of a myth" (*mythōdes*). Cf. *Agr.* 96-97; *LA* 1.43.

[32] Also see *Spec.* 1.193.

min 'ummot ha-'olam. (All the deeds of Israel are separate from those of the nations.)[33] But what is evident here, in addition to the separation of the Jews, is Philo's underlying contempt for the customs of other peoples.[34] These factors may have combined to produce an aloofness which pagans could interpret as anti-social behavior. So the Jews are attacked for being misanthropic, and Philo defends his people by proclaiming their philanthropy and their moral superiority. In the end, however, Philo perceives himself to be in an alien environment. He retreats from it into his own community--an act which further confirms the pagan's view that the Jews are misanthropic. A vicious circle thus is established. Philo's sense of spiritual superiority may have helped to preserve the Alexandrian Jews' religious identity. But, as in other times and places, the Jews of Alexandria paid a heavy price for this sense of themselves.

---

[33] *Midrash Bamidbar Rabba* 10:1, as quoted by Stern in *GLA* II, 41.

[34] Cf. the remarks of Daniel, "Anti-Semitism in the Hellenistic-Roman Period," p. 59: "Jewish authors, both of Palestine and of the Diaspora, often voice severe contempt for gentiles, even to the point of claiming that the world was created on behalf of the Jews...and that the pagan nations are 'like spittle'.... This dichotomy in Jewish thought between the 'chosen race' and the 'gentile sinners' was bitterly resented by gentiles.... By no means did all Jews share the attitude of superiority, but a sufficiently large number did so that it occasions no surprise for gentiles to respond in kind."

An Epilogue

by

Ben F. Meyer[1]

The "identity" in the title of this monograph might be clarified by horizon-analysis, specifying the poles of the inquiry. The objective pole is constituted by the meaning of the scriptures of Israel. The subjective pole is Philo himself and his closest circle of colleagues, elaborating and practicing a new hermeneutic, which aspires to measure up to the text as revelation of truth. First and foremost, then, "Jewish identity" in Philo's view derives from a universe of divine and human meaning.

Coming down a few notches from this spiritual universe, there was Philo's sphere of action, the pagan world, whose foci for Philo were Rome and Alexandria. Rome challenged him to become cosmopolitan and elicited from him his political treatises *In Flaccum* and *Legatio ad Gaium*. Alexandria challenged him to combat pagan intolerance and to forestall Jewish assimilation to the pagan world.

Finally, there was the world of Judaism, which, as Philo conceived it, stretched east to west from Rome to the Euphrates and north to south from Macedonia to Libya. The centre of this world was the earthly Jerusalem and the centre of Jerusalem, the temple. This centre, however, belonged to symbolic geography. For Philo, "centre" in the sense of "centre of interest" in the Jewish world was Alexandria. True, the city of God was

---

[1]This Epilogue is taken from a paper entitled "Monographs from the McMaster Project on Judaism and Christianity." It was delivered at the 1987 meetings of the Learned Societies of Canada.

Jerusalem, *Yerushalem*. Philo derived *yeru* from *li-re'ot* (*yir'eh*), to see, and *shalem* from *shalam*, to be at peace. "Jerusalem" in the sense of "vision of peace" was not to be sought among the regions of the earth but in the soul whose vision is clear and whose aim is contemplative peace. If in the end only God is true peace, the true Jerusalem is the soul turned toward God, and the house of God is not stone or timber but the soul ready to receive him.

Mendelson's monograph is an essay in ancient Jewish self-definition. The self-definition in question is that which Philo realized in his own person and commended to his fellow-Jews of the Diaspora. Its components were fidelity to and transformation of the great Jewish tradition. The fidelity found expression as orthodoxy and orthopraxy. That orthopraxy belonged to this self-definition will surprise no one. But contrary to a current view, according to which there were no Jewish theologians in this early period, Mendelson argues for a Philo who is theological and theologically orthodox. Nor is this orthodoxy a merely passive fidelity to the tradition. It is the pioneering and transformative moment in Philonian self-definition. How original was this?

Here it may be relevant to recall the history of ancient thought as sketched by Thomas Aquinas in the *Summa Theologiae* (part one, question 44, article 2) on whether God created prime matter. Whereas in his commentaries and earlier treatises Aquinas had maximized the achievements of both Plato and Aristotle, here he offered a dry assessment of their limits.

Ancient philosophers, he said, entered step by step--in three steps, as it turns out--into the knowledge of the truth. Step one was that of the *grossiores* who acknowledged the existence of no beings but bodies. Step two saw those arrive on the scene who distinguished substantial form and matter, which they supposed to be uncreated. They perceived that change took place in accord with the distinction of forms at the level of essence; and in accord with this insight, they considered being insofar as it was this kind of being. Such--despite their aspirations to treat being as being--were Plato and Aristotle. Step three witnessed a remarkable novelty, for now there arose those who reached the point of considering being as being (*aliqui erexerunt se ad considerandum ens in quantum est ens*).

Who were these *aliqui*? From elsewhere in Aquinas (e.g., *De Potentia*, 3.5. resp.) they were, if not Plato and Aristotle themselves, then their followers or successors (*eorum sequaces*) who learned of being from Moses' encounter with God at the burning bush.[2] These *sequaces* of the great pagans had been transformed as philosophers by meditation on the name of God in Exod. 3:14, "I am who am." The identification of God and being allowed these men to "raise themselves" to consider being as being. Aquinas was probably thinking of pre-Augustinian Neo-Platonists.

Mendelson's treatment of Philo, however, makes one wonder whether step three in Aquinas' sketch of ancient thought might not have been taken well before these Christian Neo-Platonists. What Goodenough called "the first creed in history" and what Mendelson presents as the key to "Philo's concept of orthodoxy"

---

[2]E. Gilson, *The Spirit of Mediaeval Philosophy (Gifford Lectures 1931-1932;* New York, 1940), pp. 438-41, has synthesized the data relevant to Aquinas' views.

may also establish Philo's candidature for the title of the first true metaphysician, and first truly metaphysical theologian, i.e., the first to consider being as being, precisely because he was the first to identify God and being--from the consideration that God said to Moses: *egō eimi ho ōn* (LXX Exod. 3:14).

First tell them that I am He who IS, that they may learn the difference between is and is not, and also the further lesson that no name can properly be used of Me, to whom alone existence belongs (*Mos.* 1.75).

Classical Greek thought reserved the highest place, in the whole universe of things, for the sphere of the divine (*to theion*); in Philo, however, there was no eternal scheme of things with a place of honour for God, for the actual scheme of things was not eternal but *genetos* and it would crumble into nothingness if the living God should fail to sustain it for an instant. Those who think that the world is without beginning, he said, assign God no superiority at all. Finally, affirming the providence coherent with creation, Philo makes God "Father." As in the thought of Moses-- or, as we would put it today, of the Deuteronomists--Jewish self-definition was a reflex of Jewish faith and, above all, of the Jewish affirmation of God as unique Lord: *Akoue Israēl, Kyrios ho Theos hēmōn, Kyrios heis estin*, Hear, o Israel, the Lord our God is one Lord (Deut. 6:4). Mendelson's monograph presents itself as a model study of hermeneutics, for, in retrieving Philo's way of making sense of things, it makes sense of the way Philo makes sense of things.

A. INDEX OF PHILO'S TREATISES

De Abrahamo
Abr.	22-23	108
	70	47
	99	14-15
	107	89, 117
	133-41	95
	147	6
	178-94	132-33
	200	6
	236	6
	248	91
	251	72, 118
	260	135

De Aeternitate Mundi
Aet.	7-19	40-43
	14-15	38
	20-24	45-46
	25-26	45
	74	46

De Agricultura
Agr.	51	47
	62	117
	88-89	117
	96-97	137
	97	10
	112-19	129
	131	69

De Cherubim
Cher.	40	93
	41	73
	42	134
	48	5
	91-97	137
	96	118
	99-100	20

De Confusione Linguarum
Conf.	2	136
	6	136
	70	117
	91	118
	98	7, 47
	114	29, 48
	134-35	7
	142-43	12
	181	42
	190	10

De Congressu Eruditionis Gratia
Congr.	71ff.	72
	180	72

De Vita Contemplativa
Cont.	8	117
	20	107
	30-36	85
	58-64	134-35
	59-62	95
	68	135

De Decalogo
Decal.	52-81	34
	58	42
	64-66	35
	80	36
	121-22	90, 96

Quod Deterius Potiori Insidiari Soleat
Det.	15	12
	34	98
	99	95
	102	91
	125	136
	154-55	45
	160-62	31
	167	9

Indices

Quod Deus Sit Immutabilis
Deus	17-18	17, 24, 74
	55	7
	61	4-5, 7
	61-64	4-5
	78	7
	131-35	9

De Ebrietate
Ebr.	33-34	26-27
	36-37	28
	55	27
	64	27
	80-81	28
	95	117
	110	37
	166-70	38
	193-94	27
	199	47
	199-205	38

In Flaccum
Flac.	passim	16, 139
	20-24	122
	29	117-18
	43	131
	45-46	16
	49-50	126-27
	55	115
	96	70

De Fuga et Inventione
Fug.	33-36	101-102
	54	12
	108	14
	147f.	117
	179-81	15
	180	117

De Gigantibus
Gig.	14	98
	58-60	137

Quis Rerum Divinarum Heres Sit
Her.	81	11
	169	99
	192	63
	246	43

Hypothetica
Hypoth.	7.10-14	85
	7.18-19	112

De Josepho
Jos.	32	22
	40-48	120
	43	94
	119-21	119
	151	15
	202-203	22
	240	113
	254	23

Legum Allegoriarum
LA	1.2	8
	1.5	41
	1.43	137
	1.51-52	33
	1.62	19
	2.1-3	33
	2.17	96
	2.19	10, 137
	2.19-21	10
	2.67	73
	2.103	117
	3.11	18
	3.28-31	47
	3.37-39	119
	3.67-68	97
	3.76	97
	3.107	97
	3.111	96
	3.116	97

LA	3.156	96
	3.183-84	96
	3.206	7

Legatio ad Gaium
Legat.	passim	16, 139
	115-18	33
	156-57	62
	158	60-61
	162-64	33
	166	117
	209	18
	210	130
	214	17
	281-83	16
	353	33
	361-63	70-71
	371	28

De Migratione Abrahami
Mig.	47	107
	69	33
	89	13
	89-93	15, 52, 55-56, 58
	90	24
	91	59-60
	92	21, 55
	92-93	20-21
	140	133
	202	117

De Vita Mosis
Mos.	passim	106
	1.2-3	111
	1.21-24	22
	1.28	92, 96
	1.31-32	22
	1.34	120
	1.36	121
	1.44	119
	1.59	73
	1.75	31, 142

Mos.	1.95	108, 117
	1.141	120
	1.324	16
	2.12	136
	2.17-25	129-30
	2.23	67
	2.41-42	64
	2.44	130
	2.46	51
	2.68-69	92
	2.107-108	65
	2.161-62	118
	2.193-96	32
	2.205	26
	2.215	85
	2.216	60
	2.224	64
	2.232	65
	2.270	118

De Mutatione Nominum
Mut.	11	31
	60-62	11
	138	5
	266	14

De Opificio Mundi
Op.	passim	29, 41
	1-3	135
	3	134
	7	39-42
	27	36
	89	109
	128	85
	157	136
	166	97
	170	29, 32-33
	170-71	45
	170-72	48

Op.	171	39-42, 44	
	171-72	46, 49	
	172	29	

De Plantatione
Plant.	6-7	45
	6-8	46
	35-36	15
	36	12
	62	12
	70-72	11
	108	66
	113	9
	160-64	135

De Posteritate Caini
Post.	2	117
	5	45
	156	117

De Praemiis et Poenis
Praem.	32-34	47
	162	37
	165	17

Quod Omnis Probus Liber Sit
Prob.	75	66

De Providentia
Prov.	*frag.* 1	45
	2.2-6	47
	2.64	19
	2.71	98

Quaestiones in Exodum
QE	1.10	117
	1.18	117, 129
	2.2	55, 58, 88
	2.5	26
	2.64	47

Quaestiones in Genesim
QG	3.4	96
	3.46	55, 88
	3.46-48	55
	3.47	54, 88
	3.48	56
	3.52	55-57, 88
	3.61	55, 89, 96
	3.62	109
	4.86	91
	4.88	47
	4.168	11
	4.177	117

De Sacrificiis Abelis et Caini
Sacr.	20-32	97-98
	63	62-63
	79	21

De Somniis
Somn.	1.39	2-3
	1.73	14
	1.118	15
	1.120	12-13
	1.122	101
	1.231	31
	1.233-37	4-5
	2.9	102
	2.48-77	98
	2.123-24	61
	2.250	19-20
	2.301	11

De Specialibus Legibus
Spec.	1.1-3	54-56
	1.2	119
	1.8-10	55
	1.9	88, 96
	1.19-20	36
	1.28-29	99

Spec.
	1.53	26
	1.54–57	34, 52–53
	1.67–75	18
	1.76	62
	1.97	113, 129
	1.162–256	133
	1.186	67
	1.190	108–109
	1.193	129, 137
	1.203	66
	1.211	113
	1.271–72	66
	1.273	134
	1.290	66
	1.312	133
	1.315–16	33–34
	1.316	116
	1.319–20	6
	1.324–26	49
	1.327–45	49
	2.18–23	100–101
	2.20–22	102
	2.60	85
	2.64	85
	2.65	59
	2.79	106
	2.79–81	112
	2.86–109	112
	2.145–46	63–64
	2.163	129
	2.167	107–108
	2.188	108
	2.194	67
	2.260	47
	3.6	5
	3.7–82	91
	3.8	90
	3.8–9	96
	3.11	90–91
	3.12–31	71

Spec.	3.15-16	95
	3.34-36	93
	3.39	95
	3.51	94
	3.63	91
	3.108-11	108
	3.169-77	96
	4.15	112
	4.97	102
	4.100	68
	4.100-18	68
	4.101-105	69-70
	4.149	23-24
	4.179	115-16, 128
	4.224	121
De Virtutibus		
Virt.	51	112
	82-101	112
	97-98	112
	101	112
	102-103	112
	108	113
	109	110
	110	110-11
	131-33	108
	141	107
	223	73

B. INDEX OF BIBLE, JOSEPHUS, AND OTHER JEWISH WORKS

Pentateuch
  Genesis (Gen.)

1:1f.	38-41
1:2	40
2:2	8-9
2:21	10, 137
3:8	47-48
4:15	9
6:14	136-37
8:22	40
16:1f.	72, 118-19
17:9-14	56
17:10	88
17:24-25	89
17:27	109
21	72
28:11	101
30	73
37:14	12
41:39ff.	119
45:3ff.	113

  Exodus (Exod.)

2:11-15	119
2:21	73
3:13-14	31, 141-42
12	63-64
12:1-28	64
12:35-36	119
12:43-51	64
13:3-10	64
19:10-15	92
20:14	89-90
22:27-28	13, 26
32:1-24	118

Leviticus (Lev.)
11:1-4	67-68
11:1-23	70
11:4-7	69
11:7-8	67-68
14:34-36	9
15	91
18	71
20:10	90
23:5-8	64
24:10-16	32
24:15-16	25-26

Numbers (Num.)
9:1-5	64
9:6-13	65
14:9	14
15:32-36	59
25	34
28:16-25	64
33	16

Deuteronomy (Deut.)
4:19	36
5:18	89-90
6:4	142
7:3-6	72-73
14:3-20	70
16	64
16:16	18-21
19:14	23-24
20:10-14	110-11
22:22	90
23:1f.	49
23:18-19	94

Josephus
Antiquitates Judaicae (Ant.)
4.207	25
14, 16	62

    Bellum Judaicum (BJ)
        2.280   63
        6.420ff.   63

    Contra Apionem (Apion.)
        1.209   83
        1.229   93
        1.304-11   118
        2.15-28   118
        2.237   25

Other Jewish Works
    Babylonian Talmud
        Pesachim
        64b   63

    Jubilees
        22.16   103

    Letter of Aristeas
        128-71   68
        139   103
        180-81   71

    Midrash Rabbah
        Genesis Rabbah
        61.4   72
        Numbers Rabbah
        10.1   137-38

    Pirke Avoth
        II, 1   53

    Wisdom of Solomon
        10:15-21   120
        13-15   35
        13:6   36
        14:18-20 100
        15:14-19 117
        19:13-14 121

C. INDEX OF GREEK AND LATIN AUTHORS

Agatharchides	83
Apion	83, 86, 118
Apollonius Molon	105
Apuleius	47
Aquinas	140-42
Aristotle	41, 100, 140-41
Atticus	47
Augustine	84
Clement of Alexandria	36
Damocritus	105
Demetrius (Chronographer)	73
Diodorus Siculus	87, 105-106, 111
Diogenes Laertius	47
Hecataeus	103-104
Herodotus	54-55, 87
Hesiod	40
Horace	83
Josephus	See Index B, *supra*
Justin	89
Juvenal	84
Lysimachus	118
Manetho	93
Martial	83, 87-88
Meleager	83
Origen	36
Ovid	83
Persius	83, 87
Petronius	87
Philo of Alexandria	See Index A, *supra*
Plato	4, 38, 42, 45, 98-100, 102, 134-35, 137, 140-41
Plutarch	47, 83, 131
Pompeius Trogus	83, 105
Posidonius	105
Ps.-Plutarch	47
Seneca	47, 83-84
Strabo	87-88
Tacitus	33, 84, 87, 89, 105, 109
Theophrastus	80
Xenophon	134

D. INDEX OF MODERN AUTHORS

The number of the page on which a work is cited with full title is italicized.

Alexandre, M.	*74*
Amir, Y.	*17*, 18, 20
Attridge, H. W.	*89*, 100
Belkin, S.	*90*, 91, 94
Bell, H. I.	*126-27*
Berger, P. L.	*194*
Borgen, P.	*58*
Cohen, S. J. D.	*81*
Collins, J. J.	*xii*, 18
Colson, F. H.	*xii*, 3, 15, 17, 20, 45, 47, 64, 93, 95-96, 98, 108, 111, 118
Daniel, J. L.	*81*, 88, 104, 109, 130, 138
Douglas, M.	*56*, 69
Epstein, A. L.	*1*, 30, 78
Feldman, L. H.	*12*, 81
Flusser, D.	*26*
Forkman, G.	*53*
Frankel, Z.	*25*
Gager, J. G.	*111*
Gilson, E.	*141*
Ginzberg, L.	*73*
Goldenberg, R.	*60*, 62, 83
Goodenough, E.R.	22, *26*, 27, *29*, 41, 56, 86, 93, *94*, 141
Gordis, R.	*93*
Hecht, R. D.	*58*
Heinemann, I.	*93*, 96
Herman, S. N.	*77*
James, W.	*56*
Katz, J.	*79*, 103
Lieberman, S.	*36*
Long, A. A.	*43*
Luckmann, T.	*78*
Mack, B. L.	*3*, 51
Mansfeld, J.	*43*
Marcus, R.	3, 57, *80*
Mendelson, A.	*xii*, 22, 27, 35, 38, 60, 122
Meyer, B.F.	*139-42*

Momigliano, A.	*80*
Musurillo, H. A.	*123*
Neusner, J.	*72*
Nikiprowetzky, V.	*20*
Parkes, J. W.	*119*
Radin, M.	*111*
Runia, D. T.	*38*, 47, 51
Safrai, S.	*19*, 63
Sandmel, S.	*24*, 119, 132
Scholem, G.	*55*
Segrè, A.	*121*, 125
Sevenster, J. N.	62, 81, 83, 88, 104
Sherwin-White, A. N.	*105*
Shroyer, M. J.	8, 51
Sly, D.	*94*
Smallwood, E. M.	*17*, 125
Smith, J. Z.	*30*
Stein, S.	*103*
Stern, M.	*xii, 80*, 83-84, 86-89, 93, 103, 105, 118, 125, 131, 138
Tcherikover, V. A.	*xii, 62*, 115, 123-24, 126
Verdenius, W. J.	*100*
Wardy, B.	*28, 82*
Warry, J. G.	*100*
Winston, D.	7, 25, *35*-39, 43, 47, 55, 58, 66, 72-73, 87-88, 94, *97*, 100, 108-109, 117, 120-21
Wolfson, H.A.	*29*, 32, 35, 41, 44

140001	Approaches to Ancient Judaism I	William S. Green
140002	The Traditions of Eleazar Ben Azariah	Tzvee Zahavy
140003	Persons and Institutions in Early Rabbinic Judaism	William S. Green
140004	Claude Goldsmid Montefiore on the Ancient Rabbis	Joshua B. Stein
140005	The Ecumenical Perspective and the Modernization of Jewish Religion	S. Daniel Breslauer
140006	The Sabbath-Law of Rabbi Meir	Robert Goldenberg
140007	Rabbi Tarfon	Joel Gereboff
140008	Rabban Gamaliel II	Shamai Kanter
140009	Approaches to Ancient Judaism II	William S. Green
140010	Method and Meaning in Ancient Judaism	Jacob Neusner
140011	Approaches to Ancient Judaism III	William S. Green
140012	Turning Point: Zionism and Reform Judaism	Howard R. Greenstein
140013	Buber on God and the Perfect Man	Pamela Vermes
140014	Scholastic Rabbinism	Anthony J. Saldarini
140015	Method and Meaning in Ancient Judaism II	Jacob Neusner
140016	Method and Meaning in Ancient Judaism III	Jacob Neusner
140017	Post Mishnaic Judaism in Transition	Baruch M. Bokser
140018	A History of the Mishnaic Law of Agriculture: Tractate Maaser Sheni	Peter J. Haas
140019	Mishnah's Theology of Tithing	Martin S. Jaffee
140020	The Priestly Gift in Mishnah: A Study of Tractate Terumot	Alan. J. Peck
140021	History of Judaism: The Next Ten Years	Baruch M. Bokser
140022	Ancient Synagogues	Joseph Gutmann
140023	Warrant for Genocide	Norman Cohn
140024	The Creation of the World According to Gersonides	Jacob J. Staub
140025	Two Treatises of Philo of Alexandria: A Commentary on De Gigantibus and Quod Deus Sit Immutabilis	David Winston/John Dillon
140026	A History of the Mishnaic Law of Agriculture: Kilayim	Irving Mandelbaum
140027	Approaches to Ancient Judaism IV	William S. Green
140028	Judaism in the American Humanities	Jacob Neusner
140029	Handbook of Synagogue Architecture	Marilyn Chiat
140030	The Book of Mirrors	Daniel C. Matt
140031	Ideas in Fiction: The Works of Hayim Hazaz	Warren Bargad
140032	Approaches to Ancient Judaism V	William S. Green
140033	Sectarian Law in the Dead Sea Scrolls: Courts, Testimony and the Penal Code	Lawrence H. Schiffman
140034	A History of the United Jewish Appeal: 1939-1982	Marc L. Raphael
140035	The Academic Study of Judaism	Jacob Neusner
140036	Woman Leaders in the Ancient Synagogue	Bernadette Brooten
140037	Formative Judaism: Religious, Historical, and Literary Studies	Jacob Neusner
140038	Ben Sira's View of Women: A Literary Analysis	Warren C. Trenchard
140039	Barukh Kurzweil and Modern Hebrew Literature	James S. Diamond
140040	Israeli Childhood Stories of the Sixties: Yizhar, Aloni, Shahar, Kahana-Carmon	Gideon Telpaz

140041	*Formative Judaism II: Religious, Historical, and Literary Studies*	Jacob Neusner
140042	*Judaism in the American Humanities II: Jewish Learning and the New Humanities*	Jacob Neusner
140043	*Support for the Poor in the Mishnaic Law of Agriculture: Tractate Peah*	Roger Brooks
140044	*The Sanctity of the Seventh Year: A Study of Mishnah Tractate Shebiit*	Louis E. Newman
140045	*Character and Context: Studies in the Fiction of Abramovitsh, Brenner, and Agnon*	Jeffrey Fleck
140046	*Formative Judaism III: Religious, Historical, and Literary Studies*	Jacob Neusner
140047	*Pharaoh's Counsellors: Job, Jethro, and Balaam in Rabbinic and Patristic Tradition*	Judith Baskin
140048	*The Scrolls and Christian Origins: Studies in the Jewish Background of the New Testament*	Matthew Black
140049	*Approaches to Modern Judaism I*	Marc Lee Raphael
140050	*Mysterious Encounters at Mamre and Jabbok*	William T. Miller
140051	*The Mishnah Before 70*	Jacob Neusner
140052	*Sparda by the Bitter Sea: Imperial Interaction in Western Anatolia*	Jack Martin Balcer
140053	*Hermann Cohen: The Challenge of a Religion of Reason*	William Kluback
140054	*Approaches to Judaism in Medieval Times I*	David R. Blumenthal
140055	*In the Margins of the Yerushalmi: Glosses on the English Translation*	Jacob Neusner
140056	*Approaches to Modern Judaism II*	Marc Lee Raphael
140057	*Approaches to Judaism in Medieval Times II*	David R. Blumenthal
140058	*Midrash as Literature: The Primacy of Documentary Discourse*	JacobNeusner
140059	*The Commerce of the Sacred: Mediation of the Divine Among Jews in the Graeco-Roman Diaspora*	Jack N. Lightstone
140060	*Major Trends in Formative Judaism I: Society and Symbol in Political Crisis*	Jacob Neusner
140061	*Major Trends in Formative Judaism II: Texts, Contents, and Contexts*	Jacob Neusner
140062	*A History of the Jews in Babylonia I: The Parthian Period*	Jacob Neusner
140063	*The Talmud of Babylonia: An American Translation. XXXII: Tractate Arakhin*	Jacob Neusner
140064	*Ancient Judaism: Debates and Disputes*	Jacob Neusner
140065	*Prayers Alleged to Be Jewish: An Examination of the Constitutiones Apostolorum*	David Fiensy
140066	*The Legal Methodology of Hai Gaon*	Tsvi Groner
140067	*From Mishnah to Scripture: The Problem of the Unattributed Saying*	Jacob Neusner
140068	*Halakhah in a Theological Dimension*	David Novak
140069	*From Philo to Origen: Middle Platonism in Transition*	Robert M. Berchman
140070	*In Search of Talmudic Biography: The Problem of the Attributed Saying*	Jacob Neusner

140071	*The Death of the Old and the Birth of the New: The Framework of the Book of Numbers and the Pentateuch*	Dennis T. Olson
140072	*The Talmud of Babylonia: An American Translation. XVII: Tractate Sotah*	Jacob Neusner
140073	*Understanding Seeking Faith: Essays on the Case of Judaism. Volume Two: Literature, Religion and the Social Study of Judiasm*	JacobNeusner
140074	*The Talmud of Babylonia: An American Translation. VI: Tractate Sukkah*	Jacob Neusner
140075	*Fear Not Warrior: A Study of 'al tira' Pericopes in the Hebrew Scriptures*	Edgar W. Conrad
140076	*Formative Judaism IV: Religious, Historical, and Literary Studies*	Jacob Neusner
140077	*Biblical Patterns in Modern Literature*	David H. Hirsch/ Nehama Aschkenasy
140078	*The Talmud of Babylonia: An American Translation I: Tractate Berakhot*	Jacob Neusner
140079	*Mishnah's Division of Agriculture: A History and Theology of Seder Zeraim*	Alan J. Avery-Peck
140080	*From Tradition to Imitation: The Plan and Program of Pesiqta Rabbati and Pesiqta deRab Kahana*	Jacob Neusner
140081	*The Talmud of Babylonia: An American Translation. XXIIIA: Tractate Sanhedrin, Chapters 1-3*	Jacob Neusner
140082	*Jewish Presence in T. S. Eliot and Franz Kafka*	Melvin Wilk
140083	*School, Court, Public Administration: Judaism and its Institutions in Talmudic Babylonia*	Jacob Neusner
140084	*The Talmud of Babylonia: An American Translation. XXIIIB: Tractate Sanhedrin, Chapters 4-8*	Jacob Neusner
140085	*The Bavli and Its Sources: The Question of Tradition in the Case of Tractate Sukkah*	Jacob Neusner
140086	*From Description to Conviction: Essays on the History and Theology of Judaism*	Jacob Neusner
140087	*The Talmud of Babylonia: An American Translation. XXIIIC: Tractate Sanhedrin, Chapters 9-11*	Jacob Neusner
140088	*Mishnaic Law of Blessings and Prayers: Tractate Berakhot*	Tzvee Zahavy
140089	*The Peripatetic Saying: The Problem of the Thrice-Told Tale in Talmudic Literature*	Jacob Neusner
140090	*The Talmud of Babylonia: An American Translation. XXVI: Tractate Horayot*	Martin S. Jaffee
140091	*Formative Judaism V: Religious, Historical, and Literary Studies*	Jacob Neusner
140092	*Essays on Biblical Method and Translation*	Jacob Neusner
140093	*The Integrity of Leviticus Rabbah*	Jacob Neusner
140094	*Behind the Essenes: History and Ideology of the Dead Sea Scrolls*	Philip R. Davies
140095	*Approaches to Judaism in Medieval Times, Volume III*	David R. Blumenthal

140096	The Memorized Torah: The Mnemonic System of the Mishnah	Jacob Neusner
140097	Suhrawardi's Philosophy of Illumination	Hossein Ziai
140098	Sifre to Deuteronomy: An Analytical Translation. Volume One: Pisqaot One through One Hundred Forty-Three. Debarim, Waethanan, Eqeb	Jacob Neusner
140099	Major Trends in Formative Judaism III: The Three Stages in the Formation of Judaism	Jacob Neusner
140101	Sifre to Deuteronomy: An Analytical Translation. Volume Two: Pisqaot One Hundred Forty-Four through Three Hundred Fifty-Seven. Shofetim, Ki Tese, Ki Tabo, Nesabim, Ha'azinu, Zot Habberakhah	Jacob Neusner
140102	Sifra: The Rabbinic Commentary on Leviticus	Jacob Neusner/ Roger Brooks
140103	The Human Will in Judaism	Howard Eilberg-Schwartz
140104	Genesis Rabbah: Volume 1. Genesis 1:1 to 8:14	Jacob Neusner
140105	Genesis Rabbah: Volume 2. Genesis 8:15 to 28:9	Jacob Neusner
140106	Genesis Rabbah: Volume 3. Genesis 28:10 to 50:26	Jacob Neusner
140107	First Principles of Systemic Analysis	Jacob Neusner
140108	Genesis and Judaism	Jacob Neusner
140109	The Talmud of Babylonia: An American Translation. XXXV: Tractates Meilah and Tamid	Peter J. Haas
140110	Studies in Islamic and Judaic Traditions	William Brinner/Stephen Ricks
140111	Comparative Midrash: The Plan and Program of Genesis Rabbah and Leviticus Rabbah	Jacob Neusner
140112	The Tosefta: Its Structure and its Sources	Jacob Neusner
140113	Reading and Believing	Jacob Neusner
140114	The Fathers According to Rabbi Nathan	Jacob Neusner
140115	Etymology in Early Jewish Interpretation: The Hebrew Names in Philo	Lester L. Grabbe
140116	Understanding Seeking Faith: Essays on the Case of Judaism. Volume One: Debates on Method, Reports of Results	Jacob Neusner
140117	The Talmud of Babylonia. An American Translation. VII: Tractate Besah	Alan J. Avery-Peck
140118	Sifre to Numbers: An American Translation and Explanation, Volume One: Sifre to Numbers 1-58	Jacob Neusner
140119	Sifre to Numbers: An American Translation and Explanation, Volume Two: Sifre to Numbers 59-115	Jacob Neusner
140120	Cohen and Troeltsch: Ethical Monotheistic Religion and Theory of Culture	Wendell S. Dietrich
140121	Goodenough on the History of Religion and on Judaism	Jacob Neusner/ Ernest Frerichs
140122	Pesiqta deRab Kahana I: Pisqaot One through Fourteen	Jacob Neusner
140123	Pesiqta deRab Kahana II: Pisqaot Fifteen through Twenty-Eight and Introduction to Pesiqta deRab Kahana	Jacob Neusner
140124	Sifre to Deuteronomy: Introduction	Jacob Neusner
140126	A Conceptual Commentary on Midrash Leviticus Rabbah: Value Concepts in Jewish Thought	Max Kadushin

140127	The Other Judaisms of Late Antiquity	Alan F. Segal
140128	Josephus as a Historical Source in Patristic Literature through Eusebius	Michael Hardwick
140129	Judaism: The Evidence of the Mishnah	Jacob Neusner
140131	Philo, John and Paul: New Perspectives on Judaism and Early Christianity	Peder Borgen
140132	Babylonian Witchcraft Literature	Tzvi Abusch
140133	The Making of the Mind of Judaism: The Formative Age	Jacob Neusner
140135	Why No Gospels in Talmudic Judaism?	Jacob Neusner
140136	Torah: From Scroll to Symbol Part III: Doctrine	Jacob Neusner
140137	The Systemic Analysis of Judaism	Jacob Neusner
140138	Sifra: An Analytical Translation Vol. 1	Jacob Neusner
140139	Sifra: An Analytical Translation Vol. 2	Jacob Neusner
140140	Sifra: An Analytical Translation Vol. 3	Jacob Neusner
140141	Midrash in Context: Exegesis in Formative Judaism	Jacob Neusner
140143	Oxen, Women or Citizens? Slaves in the System of Mishnah	Paul V. Flesher
140144	The Book of the Pomegranate	Elliot R. Wolfson
140145	Wrong Ways and Right Ways in the Study of Formative Judaism	Jacob Neusner
140146	Sifra in Perspective: The Documentary Comparison of the Midrashim of Ancient Judaism	Jacob Neusner
140148	Mekhilta According to Rabbi Ishmael: An Analytical Translation	Jacob Neusner
140149	The Doctrine of the Divine Name: An Introduction to Classical Kabbalistic Theology	Stephen G. Wald
140150	Water into Wine and the Beheading of John the Baptist	Roger Aus
140151	The Formation of the Jewish Intellect	Jacob Neusner
140152	Mekhilta According to Rabbi Ishmael: An Introduction to Judaism's First Scriptural Encyclopaedia	Jacob Neusner
140153	Understanding Seeking Faith. Volume Three	Jacob Neusner
140154	Mekhilta According to Rabbi Ishmael: An Analytical Translation Volume Two	Jacob Neusner
140155	Goyim: Gentiles and Israelites in Mishnah-Tosefta	Gary P. Porton
140156	A Religion of Pots and Pans?	Jacob Neusner
140157	Claude Montefiore and Christianity	Maurice Gerald Bowler
140158	Religion and the Social Sciences	Robert A. Segal
140159	Religious Writings and Religious Systems. Volume I	Jacob Neusner
140160	The Social Study of Judaism. Volume I	Jacob Neusner
140161	Philo's Jewish Identity	Alan Mendelson
140162	The Social Study of Judaism. Volume II	Jacob Neusner
140163	The Philosophical Mishnah. Volume I	Jacob Neusner
140164	Religious Writings and Religious Systems. Volume II	Jacob Neusner
140165	Josephus as an Historical Source in Patristic Literature Through Eusebius	Michael E. Hardwick

DATE DUE

DEC 1 6 2009			

HIGHSMITH   #LO-45220